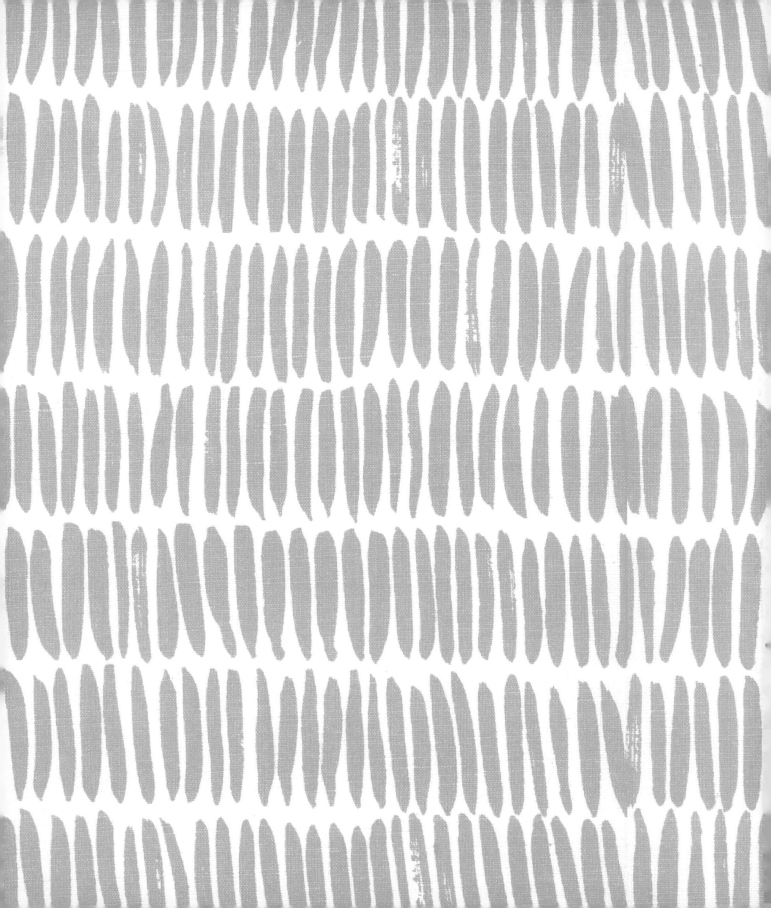

LOTTA JANSDOTTER
EVERYDAY PATTERNS

Editor: Shawna Mullen
Designer: Jenice Kim
Managing Editor: Mary O'Mara
Production Manager: Denise LaCongo

Library of Congress Control Number: 2022932896

ISBN: 978-1-4197-4398-6
eISBN: 978-1-68335-899-2

Printed and bound in China
10 9 8 7 6 5 4 3 2 1

Abrams books are available at special discounts when purchased in quantity for premiums and promotions as well as fundraising or educational use. Special editions can also be created to specification. For details, contact specialsales@abramsbooks.com or the address below.

Abrams® is a registered trademark of Harry N. Abrams, Inc.

ABRAMS The Art of Books
195 Broadway, New York, NY 10007
abramsbooks.com

LOTTA JANSDOTTER
EVERYDAY PATTERNS

easy-sew pieces to mix and match

Abrams, New York

CONTENTS

INTRODUCTION

Last spring, I had a call with my editor at Abrams, Shawna. It is always inspiring to talk together, share random stories, and laugh. In this conversation, we explored different ideas for a new book. I love creating books; I have made twelve of them now, on various subjects, but always about creativity in some way or another. And I do have many ideas still waiting—I want to make a book about printing techniques again, a big fat book of inspiration, colors, and my process as a textile designer. And perhaps a book about travel, or food—lots of ideas!

We got talking about my book *Lotta Jansdotter Everyday Style* (Abrams, 2015), a book about sewing garments for everyday activities and creating a capsule wardrobe for everyday life. That book turned out to be really popular (and is still available worldwide). It was a great deal of fun to make it, lots of hard work, but a joy. I am very proud of that book. And while talking to Shawna about it again, I realized that even though I don't sew many garments on my own, I do have lots and lots of design ideas and styling ideas I wanna

share with people all over the world who sew—and, especially, with people who are tempted to try sewing for the first time.

I started visualizing new ideas right away, many of them based on favorite looks and favorite items in my own closet, the outfits I wear most often. Above all, I wanted these new patterns to be practical and simple, yet stylish and timeless, too. Also, I thought garments that could all work together in a capsule wardrobe would be cool—and versatile.

For example, I really like wearing men's shirts in all kinds of styles, so I wanted to include a shirt pattern—and a shirt that also could become a dress is even better, so I decided to include a pattern like that. I also *really* like that the shirt is unisex—and can be worn by me, my teenage son, or my husband—so that became an inspiration when I was designing for the book: I made all of the patterns both flexible and unisex. The ideas and planning a little wardrobe came together so swiftly, I knew the timing was right.

You will see that the new patterns build on—and mix easily with—the garments in *Lotta Jansdotter Everyday Style*. The shirt dress works nicely combined and layered over the Pym Pants sewing pattern here, and also the Owyn Pants from the last book. The Esme Tunic, for example, was a hit and a favorite of many (and seeing a gazillion different Esme tunics sewn and worn on social media is SO incredibly rewarding and fun! Thank you!). But I am not surprised because tunics are awesome and versatile, I wear them all the time. So, of course, there is a new tunic pattern in this book, with a cut and style that is different than Esme . . . AND, pockets! In fact, I added pockets to almost all the garments—because pockets are the best. I don't need to spend lots of time talking about pockets . . . everyone loves them (especially in dresses).

Next, coats. I am crazy about coats and have sort of a coat addiction, so I wanted to bring in a coat pattern—this time a unisex one. I also decided to design a pattern for a fitted pant, which requires sewing skills that are a little more advanced, but the technical challenge is

so worth it. Even though I wanted to keep the focus on simplicity—my mantra is always KISS (Keep it Simple, Sweetie)—so beginners could make the garments, I think it is okay, here and there, to stretch and try some patterns aimed at the more experienced sewist, too.

The book you are reading is the result of all that designing energy: Here is a capsule wardrobe to stitch and then combine and wear in many different ways, plus lots of ideas for variations to make each garment unique. For example, the Maar Dress can be a mini or a maxi, and the long Billie Tunic can be transformed into a short version, customized with pockets and trims, or made into a unisex top. In every chapter, there are loads of combinations, outfit options, and looks.

Once again, I asked my friends and family to model the garments and I share a little bit about them. You might even recognize a few of them!

One last thing: Through the years I have received feedback from readers, which was very important to me, and helpful, too (thank you for sharing your

----

thoughts and suggestions, please keep doing that!). Taking those comments to heart, we made the pattern sheets in this book a bit less crowded so it is easier to see—and trace—each line. And we sized each pattern up one size, again, thanks to readers' feedback.

Now, I want to invite you, once again, to join me and my friends in designing and stitching garments for everyday life, whatever "everyday life" means to you— whether it means you are working in an office, cooking a shepherd's pie, traveling to Armenia, or learning how to tap dance. I hope this book inspires you to have fun creating all kinds of practical garments— for you, and for your family and friends.

—Lotta

SIX NEW GARMENTS = YOUR EASY, SMART WARDROBE

The patterns in this book are designed as a capsule wardrobe, six versatile pieces that can be combined to create options and outfits for many occasions—special everyday wear for work or play, for you, your uncle, or your mum. And yes, of course there are fun accessories to complete each look as well.

BILLIE

A top that easily becomes a tunic or a dress

RUI

The shirt that can become a dress

TOP & TUNIC

- pockets if you want

- 3/4 sleeve or short

- unisex

SHIRT

- unisex
- pockets optional

Different lengths

MAAR

A dress that can be a mini, midi, or maxi

Mini
sleeveless

Mini
capped
sleeve

DRESS

- 3/4
sleeve

- pockets
if you
want

midi

maxi

KIKO

A jacket that can become a robe or coat

JACKET
- or robe
- big pockets
- belt

PYM

The pants, a classic

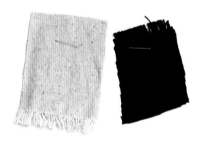

PANTS
- pockets
- buttons

- fitted high waist

- wide leg

STINA

A most useful bag in two sizes with
changeable straps

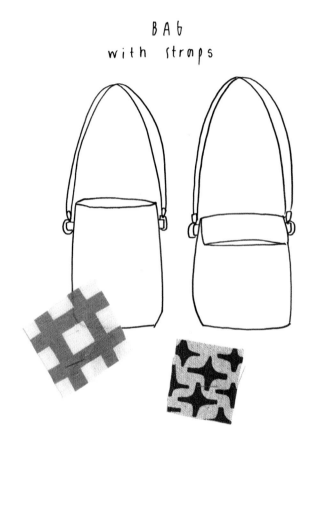

BAG
with straps

RICKIE

A skirt in different lengths

SKIRT

with or
without
pockets

whatever length
you want

CHOOOSING
FABRIC

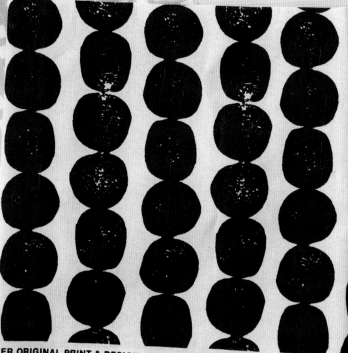

2

TER ORIGINAL PRINT & DESIGN : BERGEN © 2021 Tomma tunner skramler

As a fabric designer I get very excited about how the choice of the fabric can change the look and feeling of a garment. I really appreciate how clothing can be made festive, bold, vibrant, or playful, just by varying the pattern or color of the fabric.

That is why you will find, alongside my own pattern designs, plain and solid fabrics in these pages; because every day is not necessarily bold and festive is it? Some days one wants to be simply practical and more toned down. Having solid colors in your wardrobe adds flexibility, and, of course, nothing beats the classic black dress or black pants. So keep basics in mind when you're designing your capsule wardrobe.

All the patterned fabrics you see in the book are my own designs, printed on cotton, linen, and cotton-linen and other natural fiber fabric blends. At time of writing, they are screen printed in India and Zambia, as well as produced in North Korea (see Resources, page 144).

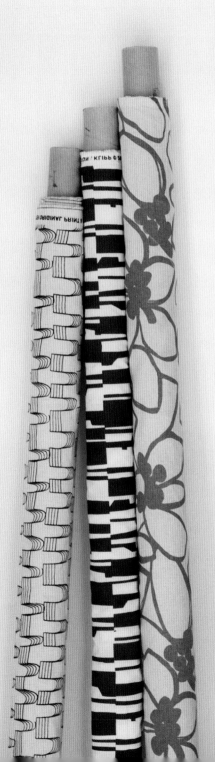

WHERE TO SOURCE FABRIC

I am lucky to live near New York City, where you can find pretty much anything your heart desires as far as fabric goes. But, even with so many options, I tend to find myself going to the same watering holes for fabric, feeling that having many, many options is not always better than a well-curated collection. (See Resources, page 144, where I list a few of my favorites.)

GETTING STARTED

While I am primarily a textile designer, I know what I like and what I think works well for my projects, including the sewing patterns in this book. Here are some basic guidelines to get you started.

If you are new to garment sewing, use a fabric that does not slip or stretch, such as cotton, linen, or a cotton-linen blend (my favorites, by the way.)

To test the garments for this book, I suggest first making them in muslin, a very cost-effective, plain weave cotton, before sewing the final garment. Once you are sure of the size and the fit, you can make them again in your "hero" fabric. Just make sure to pre-wash your hero fabric prior to sewing, to avoid surprising shrinkage later.

19

If you have never sewn a garment before, avoid silk, rayon, and shiny polyester because they slip and slide. Avoid cotton jersey and other knitted fabrics too, because the garments in this book were designed for woven materials. In general, I find that thin fabrics work best for tops and dresses; heavier fabrics are more suited to pants, skirts, and jackets.

FABRIC TYPES

COTTON

Cotton is a very versatile and comfortable fabric that comes in many different weights. Sewing with this fabric is incredibly easy. It is easy to cut, doesn't slip and slide, holds a crease, and irons nicely.

LINEN (FLAX)

Linen is a cool and absorbent fabric that is easy to sew. Like cotton, it comes in many different weights and it is often blended with other fibers (including cotton). Linen is a favorite for summer clothing and home décor. It does crease, which I personally don't mind, and requires a very hot iron to smooth wrinkles.

SILK

Silk has a smooth, soft texture that can be slippery to stitch, but feels great when worn. It is very comfortable and absorbent, but can also wrinkle easily, especially when wet. Silk is one of the strongest natural fibers, but it loses up to twenty percent of its strength if it gets wet.

WOOL

In the fabric world, the term *wool* is used for fabric made from the fiber of different animals, including sheep, goats, rabbits, alpacas, and more. Wool is strong, warm, and dry. While poorer quality wool can be coarse, high-quality wool is soft. It comes in many different weights and, although some can be washed gently in cold water, usually must be dry cleaned.

RAYON

Rayon is made from purified cellulose, primarily from wood pulp. Rayon is a versatile fiber and is widely claimed to have the same comfort properties as natural fibers. It can imitate the feel and texture of silk, wool, cotton, and linen. People do recommend dry cleaning for rayon, but you can also wash it by hand in cold water.

UPCYCLED FABRICS

Since I was a teenager, one of my favorite pastimes has been treasure hunting for fabrics at yard sales, flea markets, and thrift stores—all places to find the best, most interesting (and, often, finest quality) textiles. I spend extra time looking for curtains, tablecloths, and sheets, which can be great sources of yardage. It is good on every level (personal, environmental, and fiscal!) to repurpose discarded and unwanted fabric. Not only will you be doing the earth a favor, you will find special and unique fabrics that can then become special and unique garments just for you.

CREATING THE GARMENTS

The garments in this book are based on my own favorites, and other clothes that I wish I had in my closet. I start by drawing simple sketches, over and over again, in many different versions, to try out different styles, sleeves, lengths, and looks.

Although I love to design and create clothes, I am not a tailor, and, to be honest, neither do I sew very much. As I did my last book, I invited somebody who IS a tailor (and good at it) and I was thrilled to work with Felicity More on the drafting, pattern making, samples, and sewing instructions in these pages. She showed me so much—including all kinds of different armhole openings for tops and the best closure for the Pym Pants (buttons, not a zipper)—and she made sure the sewing patterns and instructions are all accurate and clear.

FELICITY AND ME

Felicity and I worked together in San Francisco. We met eighteen years ago, when she walked into the tiny store I had on Post Street. She was the most smiling and cheerful person then (and still is). We connected with each other immediately. And it turned out that Felicity not only drove vintage cars and motorcycles, she was an avid sewist and knitter and she also worked as a bookkeeper. Well, I truly needed to delegate that task, so she began keeping my books almost right away. A few hours of bookkeeping quickly turned into a full-time position in my studio.

Many years later, I live and work in New Jersey and Felicity lives and works in Albuquerque. But, as you know, nothing compares to seeing friends in person: It is so much more fun (and an excuse to travel and to eat that delicious New Mexican smoky green chili), so I went to visit Felicity at her Albuquerque studio to work out a few pattern ideas with her.

It was a great visit; she drove us around in her awesome 1967 vintage Alfa Romeo. It was like driving around with a big puppy—everyone stared, wanting to compliment or ask questions, often by yelling out to us on the street or in parking lots. Funny!

Felicity in her Billie Top and rolled-up canvas Pym Pants; me wearing Pym Pants in black linen and a short-sleeved Billie.

We had breakfast burritos at the Rail Yards (a farmers market downtown) one day, which also turned out to be a fabulous spot for a photo shoot. After that, we ended up on a casual, inspiring evening stroll in the mountains. It was all so lovely.

In the photos, Felicity's Pym Pants are made of a natural-colored canvas. She really likes to roll up her pants a few times, and, since most everything Felicity does, I wanna do, I did the same.

My black linen Pym Pants work really great rolled up or down, two totally different looks, which I like. My short-sleeved Billie Top is sewn in linen. I can't resist small gingham patterns and I loved the idea of having a two-sided top. Both fabrics are one hundred percent linen, which makes the top a bit wrinkly at times, but the cool kinda wrinkly, ya know? That's just what linen wants to do, get wrinkly. I don't mind it for my everyday wear, but sometimes it doesn't look super great in photos (and wrinkly linen drives photographers crazy, it turns out) so I iron it when needed. And, of course, I am wearing my favorite shoes, Sabahs. They are terrific! It is a leather shoe handcrafted in Turkey and imported by Sabah, a small company in New York (see Resources, page 144). They are super versatile and comfortable; I always wear them when I travel.

Classic, yet modern, and you can hike in them and then, later, pair them with a skirt and go out to dinner.

My Billie Top has a surprise: The back is in a contrast fabric.

Felicity Q&A, Sewing Tools and Tips
(and Where to Find Some Great Boots)

I wanted to share a few tips from Felicity about the tools she uses, how she sources fabric, and, of course, sewing techniques.

Q. How did you get started sewing? Who taught you and how old were you?

A. My grandmother sewed and knit everything she wore, and I spent many hours at the fabric shops with her and my mother. She taught me to sew when I was four or five. I had a toy hand-crank sewing machine that I would sew scraps of fabric with while she was working. When I was seven, she taught me to use patterns and sew clothes—I used a sweet floral canvas fabric to make my first wraparound skirt to wear to school.

Q. Where and when did you learn how to draft sewing patterns?

A. I took Flat Pattern Design at City College of San Francisco and learned to draft from an existing pattern—called a sloper—at half scale. We were graded on paper patterns but never sewed anything to see how it actually fit. Later, I studied with Suzy Furrer at Apparel Arts and that really opened my eyes to what was possible. We drafted a moulage (a very tight-fitting shell) to our own bodies, created our own slopers, then drafted a series of garments using the slopers. We sewed a muslin of every pattern to refine the fit. Making and sewing all those patterns in muslin showed us how important fabric grainline and seam placement are, and how something as small as a quarter of an inch can make a big difference in how well a garment fits.

Q. What kind of sewing do you enjoy doing for yourself?

A. I like to make quick, simple dresses, but I really enjoy doing hand sewing (I did a hand-tailored coat years ago) and would like to get back to that. I also knit and always have a couple projects going. I need to make a little bit every day: When I don't have time for a big project, I make beads from fabric scraps. It's a little bit of sewing, a little bit of embroidery, and a lot of happy.

Q. Which garments in the book are your favorites?

A. When I started, I was sure it would be the Pym Pants—so comfy and flattering. But now, my true favorite is the Rickie Skirt. I usually avoid gathered fabric around my waist (it makes me feel thick and poochy) but the Rickie has a yoke that is nice and flat across my belly, and then I get the benefit of a full gathered skirt. In a drapey silk it makes a great, casual all-day skirt—and you still feel dressed up if you end up somewhere fancy.

Q. When I visited your studio, I wanted that awesome lamp you have above your sewing machine, so good for detailed projects, and your Super Mist spray bottle (how did I ever do without one?) and your iron.

A. The lamp is called Stella and comes in tabletop, floor, and clamp models. The Super Mist was from a local fabric store, Hip Stitch. I use a professional, gravity-feed steam iron from Naomoto, but it is a bit of overkill for the average home sewist. I also have an Oliso® Smart Iron® for home. And I sew on a Bernina 1008.

Q. Tell me, how did you decide on that one?

A. It is the only mechanical (not electronic) machine they make, and it is a workhorse. It makes beautiful, clean stitches and I don't have to worry about the computer going on the fritz.

Q. Where do you like to shop for fabric?

A. I prefer independent stores and there are a couple here in Albuquerque—Stitchology and Hip Stitch—where I get the basics. Also, I always leave a little room in my suitcase when traveling and I search out the local fabric and yarn shops. Thrift stores can be good for finding leftover fabric or a garment that doesn't fit or has a flaw but has a full skirt with a good amount of beautiful fabric—I always buy those. A Thrifty Notion is a great online shop for secondhand fabric.

I once worked next door to Britex Fabrics in San Francisco, and I would go there on my lunch hour and just soak up all the beauty. I would wait for the twice-a-year remnant sale, which was crazy! You had to be quick and watch out for the flying elbows. I still order from the Britex online shop, as well as Purl Soho, Fancy Tiger Crafts, Cloth House London, The Fabric Store, and Tessuti Fabrics.

Here are a few tips that will make your sewing life easier: I just started using the Patterns app to catalog all my patterns, which is great when you are shopping for fabric. If you see a fabric you like, it lets you scroll through the patterns you have at home (you upload them when you get the app) and it shows you all the pertinent info—yardage, notions, etc.—so you can buy just what you need. I also use the Cora app to catalog my fabric stash.

Q. What advice would you give to somebody who has never sewn a garment before and is just starting out?

A. Find a local fabric shop and chances are they teach beginning sewing or can hook you up with a teacher. If you don't live near a fabric shop, there are many online instructions to get you started. There might also be a local sewing guild and they are always looking to convert new sewists.

Q. Any other tips for us?

A. Making the first cut into a beautiful piece of fabric can be daunting. When I'm stuck or have a hard time getting started, I find it generally boils down to fear of making a mistake. After so many years of sewing, I've realized there is no mistake that can't be fixed with a little creative thinking. Sometimes it requires walking away from it and working on something else or asking a friend to put some fresh eyes on it. I try to keep this quote, often attributed to Harry Truman, in mind: "Imperfect action is better than perfect inaction."

Q. And last, tell me about those awesome pointy short boots you're wearing with your outfit in this book. I know readers are going to ask me this question over and over again!

A. They are made by a company in Marfa, Texas, called Cobra Rock, which is owned by a charming couple.

Felicity is wearing the Billie Top (with three-quarter sleeves) made out of a double gauze fabric. This top started out with pockets, actually, but with the gauzy material they felt too bulky and it didn't really look good, so she reluctantly decided against them.

31

THE GARMENTS

BILLIE TOP AND TUNIC

When I was designing this top, I wanted to make it super simple and unisex: a top that functions like a T-shirt—classic, basic, and something that combines well with all kinds of pants and all kinds of skirts. Since I really like boat necks and think they are flattering to everyone, I added that detail as well.

With the Billie pattern, you can easily make either a classic top or a longer, tunic style. Both are easy and pull on over your head, so you do not need to know how to sew buttons, zippers, or closures. You can choose short or three-quarter-length sleeves—and you can add pockets (or have none). Because the style is so simple, you can sew it in many different textiles, fabric weights, and patterns and they will all work. Make a solid-color top, then try using a different, printed fabric to transform the look. It's addictive, you'll want to make it a hundred times over: So . . . how many will you sew? Pattern on page 98.

Billie Top: Brent

Brent is one of my oldest friends. We met in San Francisco, right after I moved there in the mid-1990s. Now, many years later, we both live on the East Coast. Brent has a deep interest in plants and gardening, and he most definitely has green thumbs. Since I recently moved to New Jersey and had absolutely no idea where to start with the garden, or how to go about planting it, I met with Brent for help. On a Saturday afternoon, he took me to one of his favorite nurseries in Brooklyn and shared much-needed insight and suggestions.

P.S. Both those plants ended up in my living room and they are still alive and doing well!

We both wore our Billie Tops and they work great together with jeans—tucked in or not. Mine is in a lightweight, 100 percent linen fabric that just gets softer with each wash.

Billie Tunic: Margareta

The local fabric store back home on the Åland Islands sells Marimekko and other Finnish fabrics. It was owned by Margareta's mum and then by Margareta (who has worked there since she was fourteen). Guess who went there to buy Marimekko dresses and meters and meters of Marimekko fabric for her projects? My mum, Mona! Of course, I had to come along, too, even as a five-year-old, and you can easily see my early inspiration as a fabric designer began with all those visits to Margareta's shop.

Margareta is a woman I have admired for many, many years, since I was a little girl on those mother-daughter shopping trips. She knows an incredible amount about Marimekko's history, designs, and collections, and about fabrics in general; I always love talking to her about it. The shop is being run by her granddaughter, so the family tradition continues now that Margareta has retired. Well, there's retired and there's retired; creative, hardworking ladies like Margareta don't ever really retire.

Margareta remains a very busy artist and maker: painting and having exhibitions, enjoying photography, and selling handmade jewelry, which she makes from leather and fish skins. Yes, fish skins!

Margareta Q & A, Fabric and Styling

Because she is a fabric expert, and also terrific at styling clothes, I asked Margareta to share some of her wisdom on color, pattern, and what-to-wear-with-what.

Q. What is the most popular color fabric people sew garments with?

A. Blue has always been, and probably always will be, the most popular fabric color there is, whether for garments or decorating. Black-and-white is also a classic; and, currently, people are curious about—and more comfortable with—yellow, and other really bright colors, especially for garment sewing.

In the past, people followed fashion trends and didn't take many risks. Now, they are much more adventurous—mixing and matching styles and colors to create a personal look. People are not trying to be in fashion anymore, they want to be unique. I think it's fantastic—a much more fun approach.

Q. Small prints or big, bold prints?

A. Each has value. Small prints are discreet (you won't stick out in the crowd) and easy to accessorize if you love to wear scarves or jewelry. Small prints in calm, neutral colors are a perfect canvas to build on. Big, bold prints make a strong, confident statement and they add personality, fun, and creativity to your wardrobe instantly.

Everyone has different comfort levels, of course. So, if you love a big, bold pattern but aren't sure about wearing it, why not make it into a bag and use it as an accessory?

Q. You chose my fabric Rustam—in gray printed on natural—for your tunic; what are some ways that you will wear it?

A. I like this print a lot; it has big personality but the neutral color and small scale of the design makes it easy to combine with other things. I love wearing it with long, striped socks—and it would also look great with polka dots and checks! Or with a long-sleeved turtleneck layered underneath and big, chunky boots, or bright yellow sneakers as footwear.

Other styling ideas: Layer it over the Maar Dress. Or try wearing it with a really long, ruffled black skirt that goes all the way to the floor: That would look supercool. (Again, especially with some chunky boots).

Q: OK, so you gotta tell us about those fabulous sunglasses you are wearing. What's the story?

A: Well, a couple of years ago I took a weekend trip to Helsinki with a few girlfriends. We all got these silly sunglasses at an outdoor market. We wore them out to a bar and had so much fun. These glasses (or any fun sunglasses) are the best icebreaker—a great way to meet people, because everyone will want to know about your sunglasses!

Billie Tunic: Jenny and Lotta

This might be my all-time favorite outfit: A tunic layered over pants (and those pants are very often jeans). And I am pretty sure this is probably Jenny's favorite outfit as well.

Jenny is one of my closest friends and we have known each other since we were ten. We have so much in common—including what we like to wear—and it makes us laugh because we buy the same things all the time: We bought the same striped tunic (of course!) at Uniqlo in Tokyo. We have the same Portuguese mesh shoes. We picked up identical Wrangler jeans on a road trip through Texas. And yes, we have the same top that we each bought at the shop Layla in Brooklyn . . . and the same clogs, that we both loved when we lived in San Francisco . . . and the same wraparound skirt that we each came away with after a visit to a marketplace in Swaziland . . . and—well, you get the idea, the list of favorite garments we have in common goes on forever.

Some of you might know that, when she is not modeling, Jenny is the photographer for many of my catalogs, magazine articles, products, workshops, and books (including this one). She and I have traveled together for more than twenty-five years and taken photos all over the world—including LOTS of selfies, even long before there was a word for *selfie*.

This tunic will (of course) work well as a dress and can be made any length that suits you best. I tend to like mine just ever so slightly below my knees

Billie Tunic: Agnetha

This is the perfect tunic for a busy day, modeled here by a woman who can do anything—from making jams, jellies, cordials, and bread, to dyeing yarn with moss and other plants and then using it to knit and crochet. She also makes baskets, leather belts, and purses, throws pots on a wheel, and even built a wheelbarrow recently. And she can sew; but even if your day is a LITTLE less busy than Agnetha's, this tunic will work beautifully.

Agnetha is my sister-in-law and we have been family since I was seven years old. She made a big impression on me the very first time we met, on Christmas Eve many years ago. She had made these cute Santa Claus figures, filled with candy and fun things, out of recycled yogurt containers, felt, and beads. Through the years, she continues to impress me with all the things she can make (she even once made me a bridesmaid dress in exchange for a twelve-pack of beer!).

Agnetha Q&A,
Why I Like to Sew . . .

(it's the best way to get garments that really *fit*)

My sister-in-law is very special to me, and she sews wonderfully. I wanted to find out more about how she got started, what tools she uses, and why she loves to sew.

Q. Who taught you to sew?

A. In Scandinavia we learn in school: everybody, boys and girls, takes sewing and knitting classes in elementary and middle school. I started sewing when I was about ten. One of the first projects I made was a fabric bag (for gym) with drawstring handles.

Q. Do you remember what your first garment was?

A. Oh, yes! When I was twelve, I made a pair of pants. I was tall for my age and was frustrated that I couldn't find pants that were long enough. Nothing fit very well, so I made my own . . . and they fit.

Q. Which garment in this book is your favorite to sew?

A. All of the patterns are pretty easy and straightforward—but the Maar Dress is extra fun to make. Adding the ruffles, figuring out the folds and the different layers, it is just a super fun challenge. (And pretty easy once you get the hang of things.) Working with your fabrics, which I love, and with you—well, that was the best part, too. It was really special.

Q. What sewing machine do you use? What other tools do you think are most important?

A. I use a PFAFF Quilt Expression 4.0. It has a really good automatic feeder, lots of stitching choices, and it is a professional grade machine—which, if you sew quite a bit, is wonderful.

For tools, a good iron is key and worth the extra money; you need your iron all the time in garment sewing. When you are shopping for an iron, look for one with a reliable steamer function that makes a steady stream of plentiful hot steam (and doesn't drip).

Next, sharp scissors are a must. After that, I love my mini thread snipper—a cute little nipper/cutter without handles. It is always right next to my sewing machine and I use it all the time. It has become one of my most important tools. You sent it to me from Japan, as part of my birthday gift when I turned forty, do you remember?

(Ah, Agnetha, I do! Thank you and I am forever grateful for all your work on this book. I am so delighted that little cutting tool is still with you.)

Agnetha helped sew many of the garments featured in this book. She continues to inspire me with her handcrafting skills and I am so grateful for all of her excellent sewing.

RUI SHIRT AND SHIRTDRESS

On to a classic: a button-down shirt. In the last few years, I have started wearing these classic shirts more and more. I like wearing them buttoned all the way up and tucked into a pair of high-waisted pants—or untucked with a big, wide skirt. I prefer patterns over solid colors, but that is simply how I like them for me.

This shirt pattern can be a bit longer—knee-length—to layer easily over pants or to wear alone as a dress. Love it. When you make the longer length, I recommend adding pockets, which are always so practical and useful. I even added pockets to a short version of Rui, which made it really cool and different, but admittedly a little harder to tuck inside pants. Play with different lengths, try all the variations—and perhaps even add a chest pocket. Print patterns and colors will change the feel and function of the Rui Shirtdress, and you'll find it becomes a staple garment in your wardrobe very quickly. Pattern on page 101.

Rui Shirtdress: Judy

When sewn in bright red linen fabric, Rui becomes a lovely, stylish dress perfect for dinner and drinks in town. When sewn as a muslin, it functions as a useful and very practical smock for working in the studio.

When I graduated from high school, I was searching for what I wanted to be "when I grew up." I knew I wanted to work with my hands doing something creative, but I didn't really know or understand how that would work and what that would look like for me. Every summer, I would visit (and I still do) Judy's *Keramik*, a small, very productive and exciting studio shop located in an old dairy. Judy has been working with clay most of her life, and on those visits, seeing her make and sell ceramics—and make a living doing it—was an incredibly important source of inspiration. Judy would meet me with the biggest smile and always offered encouragement, which meant the world.

She has not run out of those amazing smiles, and she is simply one of the most positive people I know. She still works like mad, too: At sixty-four, she is more productive than ever, always creating new shapes and more products.

I asked her to model the Rui Shirtdress, suspecting that Judy could really rock this garment and make it work in many ways, and of course she did.

Rui Shirt: Tim and Teo

Don't you love it when mistakes turn out to be great discoveries? Honestly, the pockets on this shirt were a bit of a mistake: In my original plan, this pattern wasn't meant to have pockets at all. But, once added, they turned out to be a cool, unusual feature on a men's shirt. So practical, too!

Tim and Teo love to meet for a coffee break, or *Fika*, as they say in Sweden. I was happy to tag along and hang out with some of my favorite peeps. Tim has a knack for knowing all the best spots in the city, not only for coffee, but anything that entails good food and good atmosphere. Tim is one of my closest friends and also Jenny's (page 39) husband. I have watched their son Teo grow up for the last twenty years.

Teo's shirt is short and has no pockets, so he can easily tuck it into his pants for a more formal look—or keep it untucked for a more casual style. I used a new print, called Soile, for this shirt, in a soft pink color to give it a retro, 1980s look. When Teo asked if he could have the shirt to wear after modeling it, I knew it was a great fit for him. (And yeah, I was flattered—success!) Teo is wearing the shirt in size XL; Tim's is size XXL. The unisex design is also shown on pages 88, 89, and 90.

MAAR DRESS

I wanted to include a stylish, big, bold, billowy, and fun dress that says JOY! A dress that is fun, that makes you wanna twirl and dance (or at least skip) and go to parties. But it was also important to me that the dress (and all the garments in this book) was practical enough for everyday wear, too.

I found a great solution with the maxi, midi, and mini options for the Maar Dress. Maxi is for when you wanna feel . . . well, Maxi! When you add the two extra tiers to this dress you definitely make it more of a statement. Or add a single tier for just enough extra detail. Or don't add any tiers at all and you have a great everyday dress that works anytime, anywhere.

For this dress, you also have the choice of sleeveless, cap sleeves, or three-quarter-length sleeves. All these style options allow you to create many different variations: dresses that will fit so many different moods and events. And you know that there is nothing preventing you from dancing your little tushy off in ANY of the dresses that you make. Pattern on page 107.

Maar Dress:
Ellie and Cherokee

Combining different colors together makes for very interesting, bold, and creative dresses. Color blocking gives versatility to clothing, and I think it works so well with the Maar pattern. There is really no limit to how many different and unique dresses you can create by simply using different color combinations.

One of my favorite memories with my friends Ellie and Cherokee is a brilliant, warm, May evening in Brooklyn about nine years ago. Back then, they hosted super-fun dance parties (with lessons!) on a big lawn by the waterfront in Dumbo. That evening, they were teaching Bhangra dancing and we all had brought picnic blankets, our happiest dance moves, and our little kids . . . and oh, did they dance their little hearts out together. It was joyous and incredible.

Ellie and Cherokee still live in Brooklyn and I asked them to model the Maar Dress in my old Red Hook neighborhood. I felt that a mini version in bright green would look so well on Cherokee, and a long, flowy, colorful version would suit Ellie perfectly . . . and come to think of it, both of these dresses would be great to wear on the dance floor—or lawn!

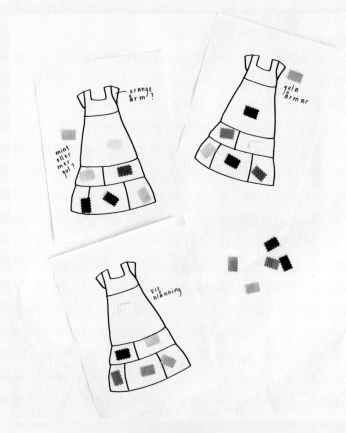

Color Combos

How do you combine colors? It might be intimidating at first, so how about looking at a color wheel for inspiration? If you are having trouble choosing, I am confident that this will help you find your own ideal combination for a color block dress.

For Ellie's dress, I chose a solid color for the body (dark blue or black are always a good foundation). After that, I added a gorgeous blue for the second color. I really liked this blue and black together, so that was my starting point. Then I played around with little fabric swatches to see what other colors felt like they wanted to be together with the blue-and-black color combo. As you can see, I actually cut out the fabric and mocked up miniature dresses, gluing the pieces down on paper. This helped me envision the finished dress and plan how much of each fabric color I would need.

For me, it feels best to limit everything to five colors, to keep the combination harmonious. Choosing a lighter-colored fabric for the body will change the mood and look of the dress completely, so play around some. You will quickly find that you can create many different kinds of dresses by simply changing color combinations.

Maar Maxi Dress and Rui Shirt: Andrew and Linnea

I visited Stockholm, where I grew up and went to school, to take many of the photos for this book. Stockholm is such a beautiful and charming city, especially the bohemian Söder neighborhood, which if full of interesting and inspiring shops, and jam-packed with excellent restaurants and coffee places. I love the architecture, the parks, the wall colors on buildings, the stone steps, and door handles.

My cousin Andrew lives in Stockholm with his girlfriend Linnea. Andrew is an artist, animator, and game designer and can illustrate the most incredible and realistic details with the computer. Linnea works at the library and likes to sew in her free time. We met in Söder for lunch and Linnea wore the long, maxi version of the Maar Dress. I designed it for her in my Yrsa fabric, a big, bold, feminine print in a rusty brick color—perfect with her red hair. That dress is simply perfect on her, like she had lived in it forever.

Maar Mini Dress: Olga

When I caught up with Olga, she had just graduated from high school in Stockholm. In Sweden you choose a major to study for three years of high school. When you graduate, it is customary to wear white and everybody gets a special graduation hat to wear during the last week of school, at graduation, and at all the parties that follow! So, this cute, white Maar mini—made in sturdy 100 percent linen—was perfect for Olga.

I prewashed the fabric in hot water before sewing, which gave it a soft texture. The heavy weight of the linen creates a wonderful drape and gives the dress great body. She looks like a real star . . . well, she IS a star.

PYM PANTS

I really like pants to come high up on my waist. Not only is this style comfortable, it's flattering: It looks as good as it feels and works for any body shape or size. Because I also need deep, functional pocket on my pants, so stuff will actually stay in my pockets, I made sure Pym Pants had both front and back pockets. (Life is full of treasures everywhere; you never know what you might find. So it's good to have many pockets and always be ready.) The pant width has a wee bit of flare, but not too much. There are buttons on each side for closure, avoiding zippers at all costs and making it a classic sailor look—one of my favorite styles.

Sewing this pattern is probably going to take a little more of your focus and time than the other garments in the book. It might take a little fidgeting and adjustment to get the perfect fit, but I assure you, you will not regret your efforts: You will LIVE in these pants. I have two basic pairs, one in a midweight canvas for a casual, work wear style that goes with any kind of top or tunic and will match in any color! I simply love my off-white canvas pants. And, of course, a classic black pair of pants is also a wardrobe essential. Mine are made in heavyweight linen, which gives the pants a totally different feel and movement than the canvas fabric pair. And I regret not making a pair of pants in a print pattern—I need to remedy that very soon. So now, I hope you play around with different fabrics, colors and prints to make your new favorite pair of pants. Pattern on page 113.

KIKO JACKET
AND ROBE

This jacket is perfect for layering; you can pretty much use it on top of any other piece of clothing to change your look and it will make your outfit instantly special and unique. Pair it with jeans, trousers, a skirt, or a dress. On cold days, try layering it over a long-sleeved turtleneck, hoodie, or Billie Top. It has a relaxed fit and is unisex, making it great for both casual wear and workwear. Add a belt if you want a more fitted look. You can also make it wild, with a bold, bright print, for a supercool party jacket. There are no buttons, so no need to worry about which side the buttons should be on. But the very best things about this jacket are the big pockets for your wallet, keys, and phone.

I suggest using mid- to heavyweight fabric to make Kiko, to give it some body and structure. I used a thick Harris Tweed for one of my jackets, for nippier autumn days. But why not also make a lovely silk jacket (or robe) to layer on top of tank tops on hot summer days? The Kiko pattern easily turns into a robe, and you can choose the length that works perfectly for you. I love to make these robes for my peeps and family: They make perfect birthday and holiday gifts. Pattern on page 118.

Tiina is wearing a shorter version in a wonderful bright color that fits her personality—and her hair—so perfectly. Mattias wears a longer version of the robe in a classic black and white.

Kiko Robe:
Tiina and Mattias

Tiina is a very talented photographer who lives and works back home on Åland, and it is through work that I met her. She is married to Mattias, and together they also run a unique and very well edited gift shop in Mariehamn. They live with their two basset hounds in a gorgeous house located right by the ocean and they are some of the most avid sauna bathers I know. They often end their workday with sauna and a swim in the brisk waters. So who better to model the Kiko Robes?

Once you begin, you will want to sew several of these robes in different print patterns, colors, and fabrics. I made a few of them for our summer house, for guests to wear when we use the sauna—because, of course, most of us are sauna enthusiasts back home on Åland. Also, these robes make great gifts. I mean, who doesn't need a bathrobe—or three?

Kiko Jacket: Boris

I was so excited when Boris agreed to model the Kiko Jacket: I made it for him in Olavi, a check fabric that is screen printed by hand—and one that I am obsessed with (which is why you see it all over this book). Kiko has a simple, minimalist shape and the unisex cut looks good on all body types. When you make it in a print pattern like Olavi, you add so much style, personality, and spice and it really becomes unique.

Here is how I wear the same jacket, but with a belt.

RICKIE SKIRT

A few years ago, while traveling in Swaziland in Africa, I bought a skirt in an open-air vegetable market. A young woman sat on an outdoor porch with her simple, old, all-metal Singer machine, making these super great skirts with a really wide waist. I was immediately drawn to them, so practical, easy-fit, and so cute—I had to have one. I wore the skirt pretty much every day and regretted not getting another five of them. After that, I decided that I needed a sewing pattern like this excellent, most perfect everyday skirt.

The whole trick, for me, is that wide waist—called a yoke, I learned. The comfortable fit reminds me of the Pym Pants: I love that high, wide waist that gives a little extra support.

The Rickie Skirt works in many different lengths; you can decide whether you are in the mood for a mini, midi, or maxi skirt. Make it in silk, cotton gauze, denim, linen, or corduroy . . . perhaps even make one that goes all the way to the ground for your next gala! Gala or not, I predict this skirt also will be your new favorite. Pattern on page 121.

I really wanted to share an outfit with high heels, but they are not my thing, and I was so happy when I could take them off! The only high heels I can wear are clogs. This outfit is completely matching, which is usually not the way to go, but I think this really works. Not only do you get a finished look, you can use the pieces as separates to pair with other garments in your closet. I really love the high-waisted yoke on the Rickie Skirt, it is so easy to wear.

Rickie Mini Skirt: Olga

Rickie is so versatile, you can wear it as a mini skirt all spring and summer, then pair it with a short jean jacket and black turtleneck for fall. In REALLY cold weather, add tights, an even bigger, chunkier sweater, and big boots—super cute, year-round.

Perhaps you remember Olga? She was a sweet twelve-year old when she modelled for my first sewing book, *Lotta Jansdotter Everyday Style*. Just as she did back then, she is modeling a skirt and sweater, but this time it is a very different kind of skirt.

To make this short version of the Rickie, I chose cotton-linen fabric in one of my very favorite fabric patterns, Redig. This big, bold print works so well for this cut and style of skirt, and the midweight fabric gives the skirt plenty of body and shape. Pattern on page 121.

I love how Olga matches her all-time favorite sneakers and gray sweater with this skirt—perfect for back-to-school fall days.

ACCESSORIES

STINA EVERYDAY TOTE BAG

I have decided to say: KISS (Keep It Simple Sweetie) instead of the other popular version of this phrase.

This is a super simple tote bag and a reminder that things don't have to be complicated or time-consuming to be good and useful. You can make many, many, great bags at almost supersonic speed using this easy pattern; some might even become gifts for friends and family.

The bag is gusseted and its size is a perfect fit for anything and everything—laptops, magazines, a water bottle, an extra sweater, your headphones, and a packet of gum (or nuts, which I always carry in my bag for that quick, little snack when I am starting to feel hangry).

The really fun part, where you can go bonkers, are the straps. You can create endless variations with different widths, trims, and color and pattern combinations. Why not stitch together scraps and leftovers from garment projects to make a patchwork strap? So much fun! I like using really heavyweight fabrics for my bags, but you can also add iron-on interfacing to give any fabric you choose a little more body and weight. Pattern on page 123.

SCARF

I design fabric and surface patterns, and what better way to show them off than in a scarf? You could not find a more super-easy sewing project. Scarves are infinitely versatile. Use one as a bandanna to tie around your neck or design a large scarf to wear and make a very different statement, much more dramatic. I also love to wrap scarves in different ways around my head. You can also roll up a big scarf and tie it around your waist as a belt. And why not try a small one around your wrist as a cute bracelet? Some people tie them to purses to make a fashion statement and add pattern and color that way. In short, scarves are the ideal small, wearable project to sew if you are a beginner, or if you don't have lots of time but feel like making something in an afternoon. Pattern on page 127.

HEADBAND

My headband is really just a scarf that has a wire in it. The sewn-in wire gives the fabric structure and flexibility, so you can make many different shapes and it will hold that form. Like everything else in the book, you can wear this headband all sorts of ways, and not only as a hair accessory. Wrap it around your neck for a stylish—and instant—accent to any outfit. Pattern on page 127.

Headband: Alejandra

Alejandra is a new friend I met last summer, back home where I spend all my summers, on the Åland Islands. She had recently moved to the same village where I have my summer house together with my little family. Alejandra is an artist and she works in many media: inks, clay, metal, and wood. She is so curious about . . . well, almost everything. She is such a bubbly bright spirit; I am so happy to have connected with such a vibrant new artist friend. I look forward to playing together with her in my summer studio, making collages, painting, working in clay, drawing, drinking a glass of wine together, and exploring many different media.

INSPIRING OUTFITS

In this chapter, I wanted to share a few garment combina-tions and styling ideas that I rely on, and that really work for me. As you can tell, I like layering. When I was pulling these outfits together, I felt very pleased and happy that it is so easy to mix garments in many combinations—just what I was aiming for when I designed the pieces, and just what you want to have in your closet when you are reaching for something to wear. Since I am a girl (an old girl now, but always a girl at heart) who leans toward a very simple and practical style, I rarely wear big jewelry or scarves—and I cannot really function in high heels at all. So I styled these the way I would wear them, and then dreamt up as many combinations as I could for added inspira-tion. What I hope is that you will find these garments easy to mix and match: Choose your own favorite colors, pick your special print patterns and fabrics, then create a unique capsule wardrobe that is the per-fect reflection of you and YOUR style.

RIGHT: This flowy, lovely, silk Rickie Skirt is all I live in during the summer. It is so easy to pair with any tops or shoes—and it is super easy and comfortable to wear.

OPPOSITE: Kiko Jacket sewn in a simple, natural-colored canvas and worn with my favorite Pym Pants in black linen. The photo was taken in a park-ing lot in Albuquerque—of all places—where Jenny, my photographer friend, found a wall that matched my outfit.

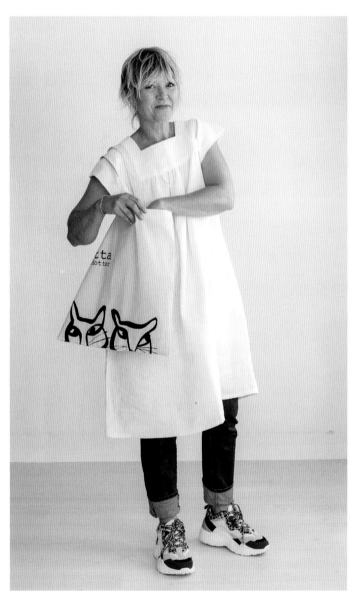
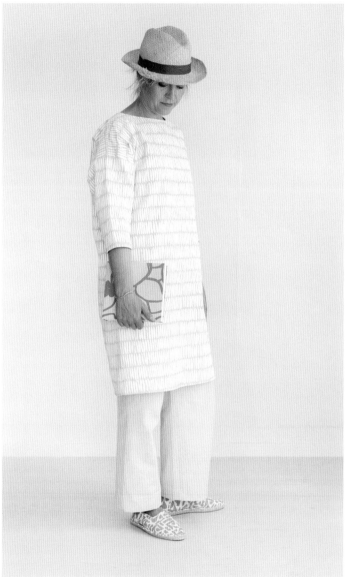

OPPOSITE, LEFT: I managed to wriggle myself into Olga's cute white dress (see page 63) to see how it would work with jeans . . . those sneakers are kinda kooky, aren't they ?

White-on-white feels like a true artist's outfit to me. I am wearing the Billie Tunic with Pym Pants opposite and at right, but see how different it feels sewn in a different colored fabric? So versatile, and I love that classic boatneck.

I really do like headbands! Mine are mostly made out of patterned fabrics, since they so easily add a bit of pop to any solid colored outfit. Mixing pattern with pattern is fun, but if you do that, pay attention to colors: black and white patterns will offset—and work great with—a more bold and vibrant color.

Here I go again, stating the obvious: when it comes to these button-down shirts, I love me some patterns. Opposite is the Rui Shirt worn with my favorite black silk Rickie Skirt and, left, a longer version of Rui that I can wear as a dress.

OPPOSITE: Well, my hair style is always sorta messy, but some days I have more bedhead than I aim for! I love big beanie hats and how easy it is to jump into a pair of linen Pym Pants and a Rui Shirt and just go and start my day, with very little fuss.

LEFT: As much as I love my Rickie Skirt in thin black silk, I also love Rickie in a thicker, sturdier fabric. It gives it a much more utilitarian look and feel. And look how those rust-colored sneakers add a great pop of color. (Love these sneakers! I scored them at a bargain outlet.) I think it is safe to say that the dark blue Billie Top will go with pretty much everything else in your closet.

More Rickie Skirts, this time in my indigo blue fabric print Olavi. Here's my favorite Billie Top again, too. I don't need to repeat that I love checked patterns: look how fabulous the little '40s armchair turned out in its new outfit. This thrift store find is a keeper. And yes, clogs, LOVE clogs, and the higher the heel the more comfortable. These are from Bryr, an all-time favorite brand, and so cute with this skirt.

SEWING INSTRUC-TIONS

The patterns for the garments in this book are located at the back in an envelope. (The two tote bags and a few accessory items do not have patterns and are made simply by following the cutting measurements in the instructions.) Identify the pattern piece required for the garment you are making in that item's instructions, then refer to the Pattern Sheet Guides on pages 130–135 for help locating which sheet your pieces are on. Trace your required pattern pieces using tracing paper, pattern paper, or tissue. Make sure to transfer all markings such as notches, darts, and placement guides. Some of the pattern pieces are divided onto more than one pattern sheet, so use the lettered and numbered matching guides, along with the outer border lines on each pattern sheet, to correctly align the sheets when tracing. You will find the Size Key on Pattern Sheet 1, inside the envelope.

GETTING STARTED

Fabric Cutting Layout

For each garment, there is a cutting layout (located on pages 128–129) to place your traced patterns on the fabric for best usage when cutting out. Black represents the right side of the fabric, white indicates the pattern piece, and a dotted pattern represents the wrong side of the pattern piece. The foldline and selvages are also marked.

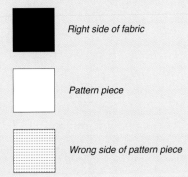

Right side of fabric

Pattern piece

Wrong side of pattern piece

Preparing Your Fabric

You should pre-treat your fabric the same as you will your finished garment (machine wash, hang dry, machine dry, dry clean). When purchasing your fabric, consider purchasing a bit more than the pattern calls for to allow for shrinkage.

Making a Muslin

It can be helpful to sew a mockup of a garment first in inexpensive fabric similar to your fashion fabric to check the fit.

SEWING TERMS

Basting

A loose, long straight stitch done either by hand or on the longest machine stitch setting. Meant to temporarily hold garment pieces together until a permanent stitch is done and then it is removed.

Bias Tape

Bias tape is made of strips of fabric cut on a 45° angle from the grainline. There are various ways to make bias tape. One simple way is to take a clear ruler and lay it on the fabric at a 45° angle from the selvedge edge, mark a line with chalk or a pencil, and draw another line parallel to that at the width your pattern calls for.

Clip Seams

Clipping into your seam allowance to—but not through—the stitching to allow a curved seam to lie flat.

Easestitch

A line of machine stitching sewn close to the stitching line within the seam allowance. Used to slightly gather fabric when the two garment pieces are uneven in length, like when you are putting a sleeve into an armhole.

Finishing Raw Edges

Finishing your raw edges in some way helps to keep the fabric from fraying and extends the life of your garment. You can do this before sewing your garment together by using your machine's zigzag or overcast stitch and going around all the edges or you can trim your seam allowances with pinking shears after sewing the seams together. If you have a serger, you can serge the seam allowances after stitching the garment together.

Slip Stitch

A hand stitch used commonly in hems or to attach a lining or facing to the inside of a garment. Take a small stitch (one or two threads) in the main fabric, then pick up a small stitch directly opposite in the facing or hem. Continue making small stitches this way every ¼" (6 mm) or so.

Stay Stitch

A line of hand or machine stitching that prevents an area from stretching once you begin sewing the garment pieces together. Stay stitching is done before you start constructing the garment and it is often one of the first things you do.

Understitch

Understitching is used to keep facings from rolling open to the right side of the garment. After clipping and pressing seams, stitch on the right side of the facing close to the seamline, being careful to catch the seam allowance underneath.

Topstitch

This is machine stitching done on the right side of the garment. While it is structural, it can also be seen as decorative and contrasting thread can be used.

Seam Allowance

All seam allowances are ½" (1.3 cm) except where noted.

Size Chart

	Bust	Waist	Hips
XSmall	32–34" / 81–86 cm	24–26" / 61–66 cm	34–36" / 86–91 cm
Small	34–36" / 86–91 cm	26–28" / 66–71 cm	36–38" / 91–97 cm
Medium	36–38" / 91–97 cm	28–30" / 71–76 cm	38–40" / 97–102 cm
Large	38–40" / 97–102 cm	30–32" / 76–81 cm	40–42" / 102–107 cm
XLarge	40–42" / 102–107 cm	32–34" / 81–86 cm	42–44" / 107–112 cm
XXLarge	42–44" / 107–112 cm	34–36" / 86–91 cm	44–46" / 112–117 cm

Tops and Dresses

BILLIE TOP AND TUNIC

Easy pullover top/tunic with pockets in two sleeve variations and two length variations.

Sleeve Variations:

Variation 1A: Short sleeve

Photos on pages 32–34, 41, 43, 75, and 82–84

Variation 1B: Short sleeve with contrasting fabrics

Photos on pages 26–28

Variation 2: Three-quarter sleeve

Photos on pages 20, 24–27, 31, 33–40, 86–87, 91–93, and 135

Supplies

- Lightweight to midweight cotton or linen
- All-purpose thread to match fabric
- ½ yard (.5 m) of fusible interfacing in a weight appropriate for your fabric
- Short sleeve, 2¼ yards (2 m) of fabric at least 45" (114 cm) wide for top; 2 3/4 yards (2.5 m) of fabric at least 45" (115 cm) wide for tunic
- Short sleeve with contrasting fabrics, 1¼ yards (1.1 m) of fabric one and 1¼ yards (1.1 m) of fabric two at least 45" (115 cm) wide for top; 1½ yards (1.4 m) of fabric one and 1½ yards (1.4 m) of fabric two at least 45" (114 cm) wide for tunic
- Three-quarter sleeve, 2½ yards (2.3 m) of fabric at least 45" (114 cm) wide for top; 3¼ yards (2.9 m) of fabric at least 45" (114 cm) wide for tunic

Tools

- Pins
- Scissors
- Water-soluble fabric marker or chalk
- Measuring tape
- Ruler

Cutting Instructions

Short Sleeve Variation 1A and Three-quarter Sleeve Variation

Pattern piece A1, front: cut one from fabric on fold

Pattern piece A2, back: cut one from fabric on fold

Pattern piece A4, front facing: cut one from fabric and cut one from interfacing

Pattern piece A5, back facing: cut one from fabric and cut one from interfacing

Pattern piece X1, pocket: cut four from fabric

Three-quarter Sleeve Variation

Pattern piece A3, three-quarter sleeve: cut two from fabric

Short Sleeve Variation 1B

Pattern piece A1, front: cut one from fabric one on fold

Pattern piece A2, back: cut one from fabric two on fold

Pattern piece A4, front facing: cut one from fabric one and cut one from interfacing

Pattern piece A5, back facing: cut one from fabric two and cut one from interfacing

Pattern piece X1, pocket: cut two from fabric one and cut two from fabric two

Refer to the Pattern Sheet Guide on page 130 to locate the pattern sheet number with the appropriate pieces for your garment. Trace the pattern pieces in your desired size and variation and place them on the fabric per the Cutting Layouts on page 128. Cut out the fabric and transfer any markings from the pattern to the fabric.

Short Sleeve Variations 1A and 1B (no pattern piece)

Cut two bias strips 1" (2.5 cm) wide x 22" (56 cm) long for binding (use either fabric for 1B)

All seam allowances are ½" (1.3 cm) unless otherwise noted.

Sewing Instructions
All Variations:

1 Following the manufacturer's instructions, fuse the interfacing to the front facing and the back facing.

2 With right sides together, sew the front facing to the back facing at the shoulder seams. Press the seam allowances open.

3 With right sides together, pin a pocket piece to the front and the back at the pocket placement notches and stitch. (If making Short Sleeve Variation 1B, stitch the pocket pieces from Fabric 1 to the front and the pocket pieces from Fabric 2 to the back.) Clip the seam allowance at the top and the bottom of pocket to, but not through, the line of stitching. Press the seam allowance towards the pocket.

4 With right sides together, pin the front and the back together at the shoulders, matching notches. Sew. Press the seam allowance open.

5 With right sides together, matching notches and shoulder seams, pin the facing to the front and back (a). Stitch using a ⅜" (1 cm) seam allowance. Clip the curves (b). Press the seam allowance towards the facing; understitch the facing. Turn the facing to the inside and press (c). Stitch the facing to the garment body in the ditch of the shoulder seam (d).

For Variation 1A and 1B:

6 With right sides together, pin the front to the back, matching notches and pockets. Stitch each side in one continuous seam, pivoting out and around pockets. Clip the seams at the underarm curve, then press the side seams open. Press the pockets toward the front.

7 With right sides together, stitch the short ends of each bias strip together to form a binding for each sleeve.

STEP 5

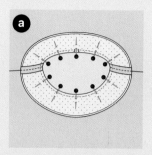

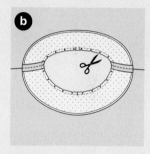

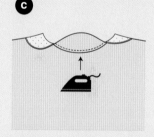

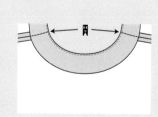

STEPS 8–9

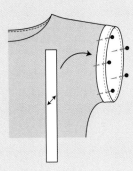

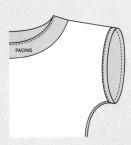

FACING

8 With right sides together, pin the bias binding to each sleeve, matching the underarm seam. Stitch using ¼" (6 mm) seam allowance. Press towards the sleeve.

9 Press under ¼" (6 mm) on the raw edge of each bias binding. Turn each to the inside and top-stitch in place.

10 Hem the garment by pressing under ½" (1.3 cm), then fold up another 1½" (4 cm) and press; pin in place. Topstitch close to the first fold.

For Variation 2:

11 With right sides together, pin each sleeve to the body, match-ing all notches. Stitch. Clip the curves. Press the seam allow-ances towards the garment body.

12 With right sides together, pin the sleeve and body together match-ing notches, underarm seams, and pockets. Starting at the sleeve opening, stitch each side in one continuous seam, pivoting out and around pockets. Clip the seams at the underarm curve. Clip above and below the pocket, then press the side seams open. Press the pockets towards the front.

13 Hem the sleeve by pressing under ½" (1.3 cm), then fold up another 1" (2.5 cm) and press; pin in place. Topstitch close to the first fold.

14 Hem the garment by pressing under ½" (1.3 cm), then fold up another 1½" (4 cm) and press; pin in place. Topstitch close to the first fold.

RUI SHIRT AND RUI SHIRTDRESS

Classic style shirt with knee- and ankle-length variations, optional pockets.

Variations

Variation 1: Shirt
Photos on pages 44, 48–49, and 88–90

Variation 2: Knee-length dress
Photos on pages 45–47

Variation 3: Ankle-length dress

Supplies

All Variations:

- Lightweight to midweight cotton or linen
- All-purpose thread to match fabric
- ½ yard (.5 m) fusible interfacing in a weight appropriate for your fabric
- ½" (1.3 cm) buttons—9 for shirt, 12 for knee-length dress, or 15 for ankle-length dress
- Button/carpet thread to match fabric (for buttons)
- Shirt, 3¼ yards (3 m) of fabric at least 45" (114 cm) wide
- Knee-length dress, 4 yards (3.6 m) of fabric at least 45" (114 cm) wide
- Ankle-length dress, 4½ yards (4.1 m) of fabric at least 45" (114 cm) wide

Tools

- Pins
- Scissors
- Water-soluble fabric marker or chalk
- Measuring tape
- Seam ripper

Cutting Instructions

All Variations:

Pattern piece B1, front: cut two from fabric; note that there are different cutting lines for the right and left front pieces

Pattern piece B2, back: cut one from fabric

Pattern piece B3, back yoke: cut two from fabric (one will be back yoke and the other will be back yoke facing)

Pattern piece X1, universal pocket: cut four from fabric

Pattern piece B4, collar stand: cut two from fabric and one from interfacing

Pattern piece B5, collar: cut two from fabric and one from interfacing

Pattern piece B6, sleeve: cut two from fabric

Pattern piece B7, sleeve placket: cut two from fabric; also cut two 1¼" x 7¼" (3 x 18.4 cm) strips of interfacing

Pattern piece B8, cuff: cut four from fabric and two from interfacing

Refer to the Pattern Sheet Guide on page 135 to locate the pattern sheet number with the appropriate pieces for your garment. Trace the pattern pieces in your desired size and variation and place them on the fabric per the Cutting Layouts on page 129. Cut out the fabric and transfer any markings from the pattern to the fabric.

All seam allowances are ½" (1.3 cm) unless noted otherwise.

STEP 2

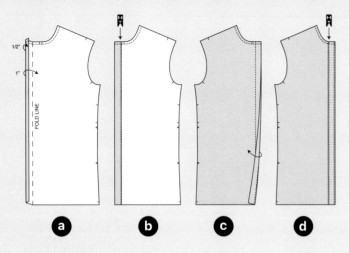

a b c d

STEP 4

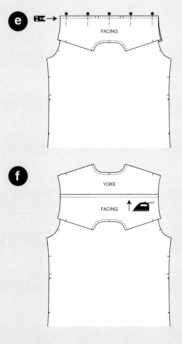

1 To prevent stretching, stay stitch the curved neck edge of each front ¼" (6 mm) from the raw edge. Stay stitch the curved neck edge of each back yoke ¼" (6 mm) from the edge.

2 On the right side of the front, press under ½" (1.3 cm), then fold under another 1" (2.5 cm) and press (a). Stitch ⅛" (3 mm) from first fold (b). Fold to the front so the stitched edge shows and press (c). Stitch the left side of placket down ⅛" (3 mm) from folded edge (d).

3 On the left side of the front, press under 1" (2.5 cm), then fold under another 1" (2.5 cm) and press. Stitch close to the first fold.

4 Place the back yoke and back yoke facing right sides together. Slide the back between the two yoke pieces and pin (e); the right side of the back should be facing the right side of the yoke. Stitch through all three thicknesses. Press the yoke piece up and leave the yoke facing piece down (f).

5 With right sides together, pin the fronts to the back yoke at the shoulders (g).

6 With the fronts still lying on top of the back, start at the bottom and roll the fronts and back up to expose the yoke facing (h). Fold the facing up to the shoulders and pin to the fronts and back yoke—the body of the garment will be rolled up between the yoke and the yoke facing (i). Stitch the shoulders through all thicknesses, making sure not to catch the body (j).

7 Reach into one armhole and pull out the garment body, turning it right side out. Press all seams. Baste across the raw edges of the neck and armholes.

8 Following the manufacturer's instructions, apply interfacing to the wrong side of one collar stand and one collar. The remaining collar stand and collar piece will be the facings.

9 With right sides together, pin the collar stand to the shirt, matching notches and placing dots at the shoulder seams; clip the neck edge of the garment as needed to pin smoothly (k). The collar stand will extend ⅜" (1 cm) past the shirt front edges. Stitch using a ⅜" (1 cm) seam allowance (l). Trim the seam (m) and press the collar stand up away from the shirt body (n).

STEPS 5–6

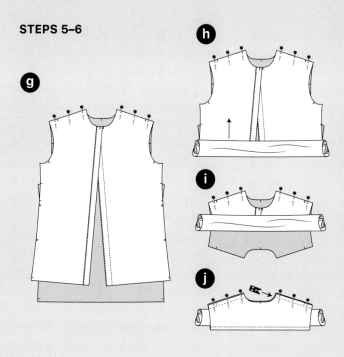

STEP 9

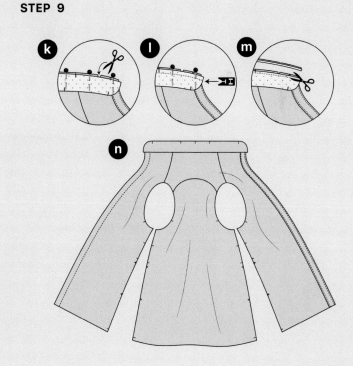

STEPS 11–13

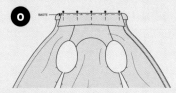

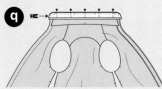

STEP 17

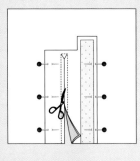

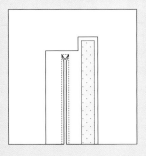

10 With right sides facing, pin the collar and collar facing together. Stitch the sides and long edge using a ⅜″ (1 cm) seam allowance, leaving the notched edge open. Clip diagonally across the stitched corners. Turn the collar right side out and press. Baste the raw edges together.

11 With right sides together, pin the collar to the collar stand, matching the center back, double notches, and dots. Baste (o).

12 Turn under ⅜″ (1 cm) on the single-notched side of the collar stand facing and press (p).

13 With right sides together, pin the collar stand facing to the collar stand matching the center back and notches; the collar is sandwiched between the collar stand pieces. Stitch through all layers using a ⅜″ (1 cm) seam allowance (q).

14 Turn the collar stand facing to the inside. Pin the pressed edge over the seam, placing the pins on the right side of the garment. Topstitch close to the edge, making sure to catch the facing on the inside. (If desired, topstitch the rest of the collar stand, working from the center back to the front on each side rather than stitching in one continuous line from front to front. This method prevents stretching the collar.)

15 Following the manufacturer's instructions, apply the strips of interfacing to the wrong sides of the long edges of the sleeve plackets.

16 Pin the right side of each placket to the wrong side of each sleeve, matching all small dots. Stitch along the stitching lines of the placket.

17 Cut each placket and sleeve on the cutting lines marked on the placket, clipping diagonally to the dots at the corners.

18 Turn each placket to the outside and press the seams towards the placket.

STEP 18

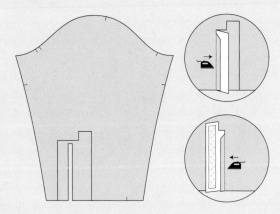

19 Press under ¼" (6 mm) on the long narrow side of each placket (r). Bring the pressed edge to the seamline, covering the seam (s). Stitch close to the folded edge to create the underlap (t).

20 Press under ¼" (6 mm) on the long edge (t) and the top edge of the other side of the placket (u).

21 Fold each placket on the marked foldline. This will create an overlap to cover the raw edges of the top of the placket and encase the seam allowance. Baste the long edge of each placket in place covering the seam allowance, making sure not to catch the pieces underneath.

22 On each placket, stitch across the short stitch line (v), pivot and stitch up the short side (w), across the top (x) and then down the long side encasing the seam allowance (y). Remove the basting stitches.

STEP 19

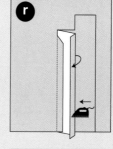

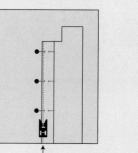

STEP 20

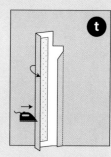

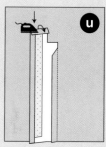

STEP 21

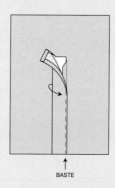

BASTE

STEP 22

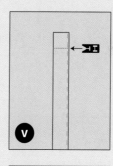

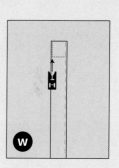

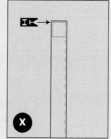

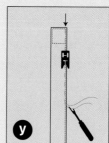

23 Make a pleat at the bottom edge of each sleeve by bringing the outer notch to the notch next to the placket. Baste across the bottom to secure each pleat.

24 With right sides together, pin each sleeve into the armhole, matching notches. Stitch. Press the seams open.

25 With right sides together, pin one pocket piece to each side of the front and the back at the placement notches. Stitch and press the pocket over the seam allowances.

26 With right sides together, pin the front to the back, matching underarm seams, notches, and pockets. Stitch in one continuous seam, pivoting out and around pockets. Clip above and below the pocket, then press the side seams open. Press the pocket toward the front.

27 Following the manufacturer's instructions, apply interfacing to a left and right cuff piece. The other two pieces will become the facings.

28 With right sides together, pin a cuff to each sleeve opening, matching the notch. The short edges will extend ½" (1.3 cm) from each side of the sleeve opening. Stitch. Press the cuff over the seam allowances.

29 Press under ½" (1.3 cm) on the notched edge of the cuff facing.

30 With right sides together, pin the cuff facing to each cuff, matching raw edges. Stitch. Clip the corners diagonally.

31 Turn each cuff right side out and press. Pin the pressed edge over the seam, placing the pins on the right side of the garment. Topstitch close to the edge, making sure to catch the facing on the inside. When worn, the cuffs may be folded back onto the sleeve if desired.

32 To hem any variation of the shirt/dress, press under ½" (1.3 cm), then fold up another 1" (2.5 cm) and press. Stitch close to the first fold.

33 Following your machine's instructions and using the buttonhole guide for your size, make buttonholes at the marked spots on the right front of the shirt/dress and also on the marked spot on each cuff.

34 Sew on the buttons, using the button/carpet thread.

MAAR DRESS

Loose-fitting dress with square neckline in three sleeve variations and three length variations—mini, midi, and maxi. The midi- and maxi-length dresses are created by adding one or two tiers of ruffles.

Sleeve Variations:

Variation 1: Sleeveless
Photos on pages 57–59

Variation 2: Cap sleeve
Photos on pages 55, 57–58, 60–63, and 86

Variation 3: Three-quarter sleeve
Photos on pages 50–53

Supplies

- Lightweight to midweight cotton or linen
- All-purpose thread to match fabric
- 1 yard (.9 m) of fusible interfacing in a weight appropriate for your fabric
- Sleeveless, 2¾ (2.5 m) yards of fabric at least 45" (114 cm) wide for mini; 3½ (3.2 m) yards of fabric at least 45" (114 cm) wide for midi; and 5 yards (4.6 m) of fabric at least 45" (114 cm) wide for maxi
- Cap sleeve, 3 yards (2.7 m) of fabric at least 45" (114 cm) wide for mini; 3¾ yards (3.4 m) of fabric at least 45" (114 cm) wide for midi; and 5¼ (4.8 m) yards of fabric at least 45" (114 cm) wide for maxi
- Three-quarter sleeve, 3¼ (3 m) yards of fabric at least 45" (114 cm) wide for mini; 4 yards (3.7 m) of fabric at least 45" (114 cm) wide for midi; and 5½ yards (5 m) of fabric at least 45" (114 cm) wide for maxi

Tools

- Pins
- Scissors
- Water-soluble fabric marker or chalk
- Measuring tape

Cutting Instructions

All Variations:

Pattern piece C1, front: cut one from fabric on fold

Pattern piece C2, back: cut one from fabric on fold

Pattern piece X1, pocket: cut four from fabric

Pattern piece C3, front yoke: cut two from fabric (one will be front yoke and the other will be front yoke facing) and cut one from interfacing

Pattern piece C4, back yoke: cut two from fabric (one will be back yoke and the other will be back yoke facing) and cut one from interfacing

Sleeveless Variation:

Pattern piece C5, armhole facing: cut two from fabric

Cap Sleeve Variation:

Pattern piece C6, cap sleeve: cut two from fabric

Three-quarter Sleeve Variation:

Pattern piece C7, three-quarter sleeve: cut two from fabric
Pattern piece C5, armhole facing: cut two from fabric

Refer to the Pattern Sheet Guide on page 134 to locate the pattern sheet number with the appropriate pieces for your garment. Trace the pattern pieces in your desired size and variation and place them on the fabric per the Cutting Layouts on page 128. Cut out the fabric and transfer any markings from the pattern to the fabric.

Ruffles for midi length (no pattern piece): cut as instructed below.

For 45"- (114 cm-) wide fabric, cut three pieces each in the following dimensions
XS - 9" x 31" (23 x 79 cm)
S - 9" x 33" (23 x 84 cm)
M - 9" x 34" (23 x 86 cm)
L - 9" x 35" (23 x 89 cm)
XL - 9" x 36" (23 x 91 cm)

Ruffles for maxi length (no pattern piece): cut pieces for midi length as above in addition to the pieces below.

For 45"- (114 cm-) wide fabric, cut four pieces each in the following dimensions
XS - 14" x 36" (35.5 x 91 cm)
S - 14" x 37" (35.5 x 94 cm)
M - 14" x 38" (35.5 x 97 cm)
L - 14" x 39" (35.5 x 99 cm)
XL - 14" x 40" (35.5 x 102 cm)
Note: To make a two-tiered multi-colored ruffle as on the maxi-length version Ellie is wearing on page 57, divide the pieces listed above into your desired number of colors—it may help to make a sketch as there are varied sizes of color blocks in this version. Be sure to add 1" (2.5 cm) for seam allowance to the length of each panel. Sew the 9" (23 cm) color blocks together into a long loop and repeat with the 14" (35.5 cm) color blocks. Set both loops aside until step 31.

All seam allowances are ½" (1.3 cm) unless noted otherwise.

Sewing Instructions
All Variations:

1 Following the manufacturer's instructions, fuse the interfacing to the wrong side of the front yoke facing and the back yoke facing.

2 With right sides together, pin a pocket piece to the side seams of the front and the back at the pocket placement notches. Stitch. Press the seam allowance toward the pocket.

3 With right sides together, pin the front and back together at the sides, matching notches and aligning pockets. Stitch down one side to the pocket, pivot and stitch around the pocket to the side seam, then pivot and stitch down to the bottom. Repeat for the other side. Clip above and below the pocket, then press the side seams open. Press the pocket toward the front.

4 Machine baste a line of gathering stitches ⅜" (1 cm) from the top edge of the front and the back, then gather the upper edges.

5 Matching notches and adjusting the gathers evenly, pin the front yoke to the front and stitch. Repeat with the back yoke and back. Press each seam allowance towards the yoke.

For Variation 1:

6 With right sides together, sew the armhole facings to the front and back yoke facing, matching the marks. Press the seams open. Press up the seam allowance on each yoke facing.

7 With right sides together, pin the yoke facing to the yoke around the front and back necklines and armholes, matching notches. Starting 2" (5 cm) down from the shoulder at the dot, stitch down one neckline, across and up the other side, stopping 2" (5 cm) from the shoulder at the dot. Repeat on the remaining neckline. Clip the corners to (but not through) the line of stitching.

8 Starting 2" (5 cm) down from one shoulder at the dot, stitch the armhole opening, stopping 2" (5 cm) from the other shoulder at the dot. Repeat on the other armhole. Clip the underarm curves.

9 Turn the facing right side out. Press the neckline and understitch the yoke facing along the neck edge only.

STEP 2

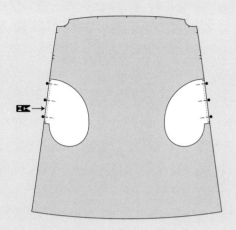

STEP 6

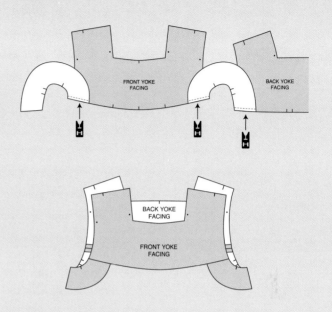

STEP 7

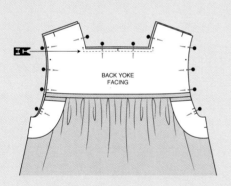

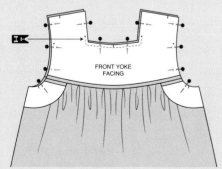

STEP 8

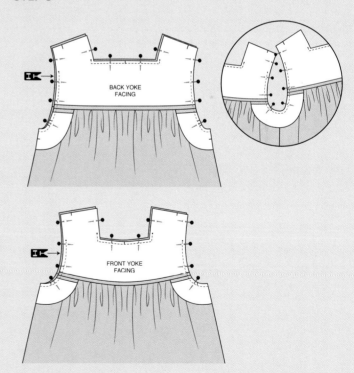

STEP 10

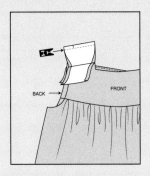

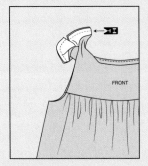

STEP 11

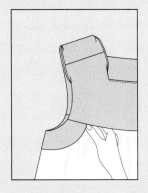

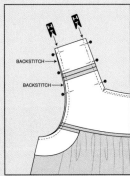

10 This step is a little tricky: with right sides together, stitch each shoulder of the front yoke facing to the shoulder of the corresponding back yoke facing. Move the facing shoulder seams out of the way, then twist the front yoke and back yoke shoulders so they are right sides together and stitch. Repeat for the second shoulder seam. Press all shoulder seams open.

11 Turn the garment inside out. Reach in between the garment and the facing to one shoulder and pull it through and inside out so you can access the unsewn shoulder and neckline seams. Match the shoulder seams and pin the open shoulder and neckline. Starting on top of the existing line of stitching, stitch both the shoulder and the neckline seams, being careful not to catch the rest of the armhole that was pulled into the shoulder. Backstitch at the beginning and end to secure. Repeat for the other side. Pull the shoulders back into place and press.

12 Pin the yoke facing to the yoke at the lower edge, covering the seam allowances. Slipstitch in place.

For Variation 2:

13 With right sides together, pin the front yoke to the back yoke at the shoulder seams, matching notches. Stitch. Press the seams open.

14 With right sides together, pin the front yoke facing to the back yoke facing at the shoulder seams and stitch. Press the shoulder seams open. Press under ½" (1.3 cm) on the lower edges of the yoke facings and press.

15 With right sides together, pin the facing to the yoke, matching shoulder seams and notches. Stitch all around the neckline, pivoting at the corners. Clip to (but not through) the stitching at the corners.

16 Turn the yoke facing to the inside and press. Understitch the yoke facing along the neckline edge only.

17 With right sides together, stitch each sleeve seam. Clip the center curve. Press the seams open. With wrong sides together, fold each sleeve in half and press, then open back up. Press one edge of each sleeve under ½" (1.3 cm).

18 With right sides together, pin the raw edge of the sleeves to the armholes, matching the underarm seams to the side seams and matching the notches to the shoulder seam, keeping the other sleeve edge free. Baste. Stitch. Stitch again ¼" (6 mm) away inside the seam allowance. Clip the curves. Press the seam allowance toward the sleeve.

19 Fold the sleeve along the pressed foldline and pin, covering the seam allowances. Slipstitch in place around the armholes.

For Variation 3:

20 Follow step 6 of Variation 1.

21 Follow steps 13–16 of Variation 2.

22 With right sides together, stitch each sleeve seam. Press the seams open. Easestitch the upper edge of each sleeve between the dots.

23 With right sides together, pin the sleeves to the armholes, matching the underarm seam to the side seams, matching double notches, and matching single notches to the shoulder seam, keeping the yoke facing free. Adjust the ease in the shoulder cap to fit and baste. Stitch. Stitch again ¼" (6 mm) away

STEP 18

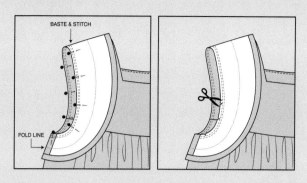

STEP 19

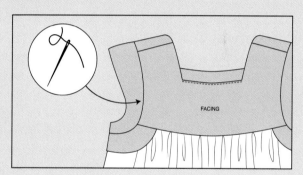

inside the seam allowance. Clip the curves. Press the seam allowances towards the yoke.

24 To hem the sleeves, press under ½" (1.3 cm), then another 1" (2.5 cm) and press. Topstitch close to the first fold.

25 Pin the yoke facings to the yoke, covering the seam allowances. Slipstitch in place at the lower edge and around the armholes.

For Variations 1, 2, and 3, mini length:

26 Press under ½" (1.3 cm) at the lower edge. Turn up another 1" (2.5 cm) and press. Stitch close to the first fold.

For Variations 1, 2, and 3, midi length:

27 With right sides together, sew the two (or three) panels together on the 9" (23 cm) sides to make a large loop. To gather the ruffle evenly, fold the long length into quarters and make a mark with a pin or tailor's chalk at each quarter. (If you're using two panels, each seam can be a mark and the midway point between the two seams would be the other mark.)

28 Use a different color thread in the bobbin for this step, as it can be helpful to keep track of which thread to pull. Gather each panel separately as follows, using a long basting stitch: stitch ¼" (6 mm) from the top edge from one seam to the next. Get as close as possible to the seam, leave the needle in the fabric, pivot away from edge, make another stitch, leave the needle in the fabric and pivot back toward the beginning. Stitch back in the opposite direction, ¼" (6 mm) away from first line of stitching. Leave a long thread tail. Repeat for each panel. Pull the bobbin threads to gather.

29 With right sides together, pin the ruffle to the bottom of the dress, matching the side seams, and match the midway marks to the center front and center back of the dress. Adjust the gathers evenly around. Stitch using a ⅝" (1.5 cm) seam allowance.

30 Press under ½" (1.3 cm) at the lower edge of the ruffle. Turn up another ½" (1.3 cm) and press. Stitch close to the first fold.

For Variations 1, 2, and 3, maxi length:

31 Follow steps 27 and 28 to create the first tier of ruffles. Then create the second tier of ruffles using the 14" (35.5 cm) tall panels, also following steps 27 and 28, but using three or four panels as indicated in the cutting instructions. (Note: If you're making the multi-color ruffle variation, use the 9" [23 cm] and 14" [35.5 cm] loops you have already constructed when gathering the ruffles in steps 27 and 28.)

32 With right sides together, pin the 9" (23 cm) tall ruffle to the bottom of the dress, matching the side seams (or quarter marks) and the midway marks to the center front and center back of the dress. Adjust the gathers evenly around. Stitch using a ⅝" (1.5 cm) seam allowance.

33 With right sides together, pin the 14" (35.5 cm) tall ruffle to the bottom of the first ruffle, matching the side seams (or quarter marks) and the midway marks to the center front and center back of the dress. Adjust the gathers evenly around. Stitch using a ⅝" (1.5 cm) seam allowance.

34 Press under ½" (1.3 cm) at the lower edge of the ruffle. Turn up another ½" (1.3 cm) and press. Stitch close to the first fold.

Bottoms and Jackets

PYM PANTS

Side-button pant, fitted at the waist and flaring into a full leg below the hip.

Photos on pages 27, 28–29, 31, 32, 64–65, 67, 82–83, 85, 86–87, 90, and 136

Supplies

- Midweight to heavyweight cotton or linen, midweight denim
- All-purpose thread to match fabric
- Ten ¾" (2 cm) buttons
- Button/carpet thread to match fabric (for buttons)
- 2¾ yards (2.5 m) of fabric at least 45" (114 cm) wide
- ½ yard (.5 m) of fusible interfacing in a weight appropriate for your fabric

Tools

- Pins
- Scissors
- Water-soluble fabric marker or chalk
- Measuring tape
- Seam ripper

Cutting Instructions

Pattern piece F1, front: cut two from fabric

Pattern piece F2, back: cut two from fabric

Pattern piece F3, back button placket: cut two from fabric and two from interfacing

Pattern piece F4, front facing: cut two from fabric and two from interfacing

Pattern piece F5, front pocket: cut two from fabric

Pattern piece F6, back pocket: cut two from fabric

Pattern piece F7, waistband front: cut two from fabric and one from interfacing (one will be the front waistband, the other will be the front waistband facing)

Pattern piece F8, waistband back: cut two from fabric and one from interfacing (one will be the back waistband, the other will be the back waistband facing)

Refer to the Pattern Sheet Guide on page 132 to locate the pattern sheet number with the appropriate pieces for your garment. Trace the pattern pieces in your desired size and place them on the fabric per the Cutting Layouts on page 128. Cut out the fabric and transfer any markings from the pattern to the fabric.

All seam allowances are ½" (1.3 cm) unless noted otherwise.

STEP 4

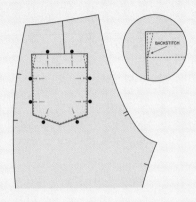

BACKSTITCH

STEP 9

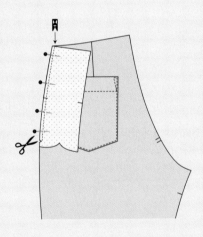

Sewing Instructions

1 Stitch the darts on the back pieces and press towards the center.

2 Fold under ½" (1.3 cm) on the top edge of each back pocket, then press under an additional 1¾" (4.5 cm). Topstitch each pocket close to the first fold.

3 Fold under ½" (1.3 cm) on each side of both pockets and press. Then fold under a ½" (1.3 cm) hem on the bottom edges of each pocket and press.

4 Pin the pockets to the pant backs, placing the top corners at the dots. Topstitch in place along the sides and lower edge, backstitching at the beginning and end to secure. To reinforce the pockets, topstitch the corners as shown. Backstitch to secure.

5 To reinforce the opening for the front pocket, cut a piece of interfacing 1" (2.5 cm) wide by the length of the angled front edge of the pocket. Following the manufacturer's instructions, apply the interfacing to the seam allowance of the angled pocket edge; add a line of zigzag stitching along this angled edge to reinforce.

Fold under ½" (1.3 cm) on the front opening, press, and topstitch ⅜" (1 cm) from the folded edge. Repeat for the second pocket.

6 Press under ½" (1.3 cm) on the long and short sides of each pocket, then press under a ½" (1.3 cm) hem on the bottom edge of each pocket.

7 Pin the pockets to the pant fronts, matching all notches and marks. Topstitch in place along the sides and lower edge, backstitching at the beginning and end to secure. Baste across the top of the pocket.

8 Following the manufacturer's instructions, apply interfacing to each back button placket. Fold each placket in half lengthwise, wrong sides together. Press. Unfold each placket to continue.

9 With right sides together, pin a placket to one side of the back, matching notches. Stitch using a ¼" (6 mm) seam allowance, stopping at the dot. Clip to, but not through, the seam allowance at the dot. Press the placket over the seam allowance. Repeat for the second placket.

10 Press under ¼" (6 mm) on the raw edge of one placket. Fold the placket in half along the pressed foldline and pin, making sure to cover the seam. Topstitch the placket ⅛" (3 mm) from the folded edge. Stitch the bottom of the placket closed using a zig-zag stitch. Repeat for the other placket. Press each placket away from the back.

11 Following the manufacturer's instructions, apply the interfacing to the wrong sides of the front facing pieces. Finish the shorter side and curved bottom edge of the facing with a zigzag stitch. With right sides together, pin the longer straight side of the front facing to the pant front, matching the dots. Stitch in a ½" (1.3 cm) seam. Clip to, but not through, the seam allowance at the dot. Press the facing to the inside. Topstitch 1⅝" (4.2 cm) from the edge.

12 With right sides together, pin the front and back together at one side, matching notches. Stitch beginning at the dot, making sure not to catch the edge of the pocket on the front or the placket on the back (a). Press the seam open. Repeat for the other side (b).

STEP 12

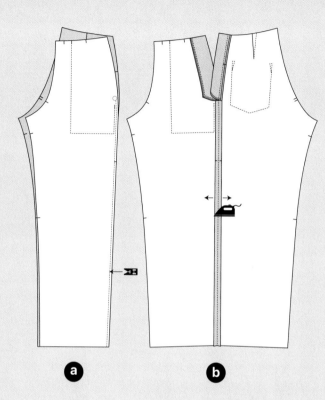

115

STEP 13

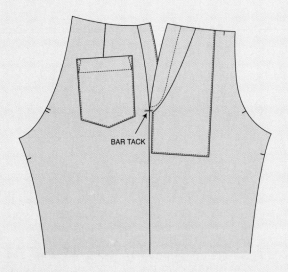

BAR TACK

STEP 15

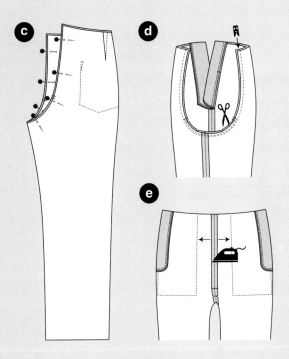

13 To reinforce the bottom of the front opening, make a bar tack (a few back-and-forth topstitches) at the point where the front and back meet.

14 With right sides together, pin the front and the back together, matching notches. Stitch the inner leg seams. Clip the seam at the curve at the thighs. Press the seams open.

15 With the pant still inside out, place one leg inside the other so they are right sides together. Pin the front to the back, matching the notches and seams (c). Stitch. Sew another line of stitching ¼" (6 mm) inside the seam allowance at the crotch curve to reinforce this area. Clip the curves (d). Remove the leg that is inside the other. Press the seam open on either side of the rein-forced area (e).

16 Following the manufacturer's instructions, fuse the interfacing to the waistband front and the waistband back. With right sides together, pin the waistband front to the pant front, matching the centers; note that the waistband will extend ½" (1.3 cm) beyond the pant front on each side. Stitch. Clip the seam and press the waist-band away from the pant. Repeat for the back waistband.

17 Press under ½" (1.3 cm) on the long raw edge of each waistband facing. With right sides together, pin the front waistband facing to the front waistband, placing the pressed edge at the seamline. Stitch from one short side to the other, backstitching at the beginning and end to secure. Clip the corners diagonally and trim the seam allowances on the short sides to ¼" (6 mm). Turn the waistband right side out. Press. Repeat for the back waistband.

18 Pin the waistband facing over the seam allowance. Slip stitch in place by hand or topstitch with the machine.

19 To hem each leg, press under ¼" (6 mm) and then fold up another 1½" (4 cm) and press. Topstitch close to the first fold.

20 Using the front facing and front waistband as a template, mark buttonholes onto the pant fronts. Following your machine's instructions, make buttonholes on the pant front at the markings. Sew on the buttons, using the button/carpet thread.

STEP 17

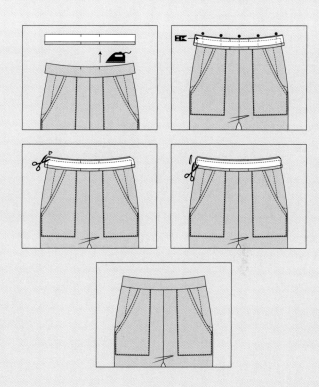

KIKO JACKET AND ROBE

Simple unlined jacket with pockets, in three length variations and with an optional belt.

Variations

Variation 1: Hip-length jacket
Photos on pages 66–67 and 70–71

Variation 2: Knee-length robe
Photos on page 68–69

Variation 3: Ankle-length robe
Photos on page 68–69

Supplies
All Variations:

- Lightweight to midweight cotton or linen for robe, midweight to heavyweight cotton or linen for jacket
- All-purpose thread to match fabric
- Jacket, 3 yards (2.7 m) of fabric at least 45" (114 cm) wide
- Knee-length robe, 3¾ yards (3.4 m) of fabric at least 45" (114 cm) wide
- Ankle-length robe, 4½ yards (4 m) of fabric at least 45" (114 cm) wide

Tools
- Pins
- Scissors
- Water-soluble fabric marker or chalk
- Measuring tape
- Chopstick or knitting needle (optional)

Cutting Instructions
All Variations:

Pattern piece E1, front: cut two from fabric
Pattern piece E2, back: cut one from fabric on fold
Pattern piece E3, sleeve: cut two from fabric
Pattern piece E4, pocket: cut two from fabric

Refer to the Pattern Sheet Guide on page 131 to locate the pattern sheet number with the appropriate pieces for your garment. Trace the pattern pieces in your desired size and variation and place them on the fabric per the Cutting Layouts on pages 128–129. Cut out the fabric and transfer any markings from the pattern to the fabric.

Collar band (no pattern piece): cut two strips to the dimensions given below.

XS – 5" (13 cm) x 31¼" (79 cm) for jacket, 43¼" (109.9 cm) for knee length, 55¼" (140 cm) for long length
S – 5" (13 cm) x 32¼" (82 cm) for jacket, 44½" (113 cm) for knee length, 57" (144.8 cm) for long length

M – 5" (13 cm) x 33" (83.8 cm) for jacket, 45½" (115.6 cm) for knee length, 58" (147.3 cm) for long length

L – 5" (13 cm) x 33¾" (85.7 cm) for jacket, 46¾" (118.7 cm) for knee length, 59½" (151 cm) for long length
XL – 5" (13 cm) x 34½" (87.6 cm) for jacket, 47½" (120.7 cm) for knee length, 60½" (153.7 cm) for long length

Belt (no pattern piece): To determine how long to cut the belt piece, take a length of cord or ribbon and tie it around your waist. Decide how long you want the ties to hang and cut the cord to the appropriate length. Measure the cord, add 1" (2.5 cm) for seam allowance and 5–9" (13 to 23 cm) for the knot, depending on how heavy your fabric is (5" [13 cm] for lightweight fabrics, 9" [23 cm] for heavier fabrics).

Cut one strip of fabric 5" (13 cm) wide by your desired length. For example, the finished length of the belt for the jacket shown here was 58" (147 cm) long, so the strip was cut to 5" x 59" (13 cm x 149.9 cm).

All seam allowances are ½" (1.3 cm) unless noted otherwise.

Sewing Instructions
For Variations 2 and 3:

1 Fold under ½″ (1.3 cm) on the top edge of the pocket and press. Fold under another 2″ (5 cm) and press. Topstitch close to the first fold. Fold under ½″ (1.3 cm) on the sides and bottom of the pocket and press.

2 Pin a pocket to each front at the markings. Topstitch in place along the sides and lower edge, back-stitching at the beginning and end to secure.

3 With right sides together, stitch the fronts to the back at the shoulder. Press the seams open.

4 With right sides together, pin each sleeve to the front/back, matching the shoulder seam to the notch on sleeve, and stitch. Press the seam towards the sleeve.

5 With right sides together, pin the garment together and sew the sleeve seams and robe side seams in one continuous seam. Clip at the underarm curve. Press the seam open.

STEP 3

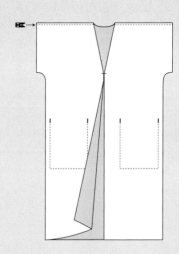

STEP 5

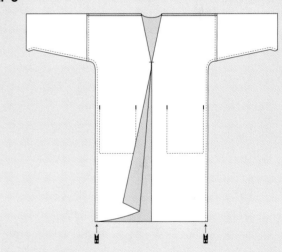

119

STEP 9

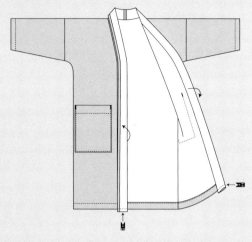

STEP 11

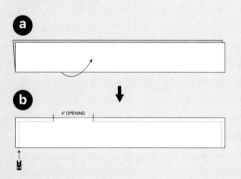

6 To hem the sleeves, fold under ½" (1.3 cm) and press, then fold under another 1" (2.5 cm) and press. On the right side, topstitch close to the first fold, being sure to catch the hem underneath.

7 To hem the robe, fold under ½" (1.3 cm), then fold under another 1" (2.5 cm) and press. Topstitch close to the first fold.

8 With right sides together, sew one short end of the collar band pieces together. Press the seam open. Press under ½" (1.3 cm) on one long raw edge of the collar band. With right sides together, pin the remaining long edge of the collar to the robe, matching the collar band seam to the center back; note that it will extend ½" (1.3 cm) or a bit more beyond the bottom edge. Stitch. Press the collar band away from the body.

9 Fold the lower edge of collar band so the right sides are facing, matching the pressed edge to the seamline. Stitch across the bottom. Trim the seam allowance and clip the corner diagonally to reduce bulk. Turn the band right side out and press.

10 Fold the collar band over the seamline and pin in place. Topstitch close to the pressed edge, being sure to catch the folded edge as you sew.

11 To make the belt, fold the cut strip in half lengthwise, right sides together (a). Stitch along each short end and along the long edge, leaving a 4" (10 cm) opening in the long edge to turn (b). Clip the corners diagonally. Turn the belt right side out—a chopstick or knitting needle can be helpful to push the corners out. Press. Machine stitch the 4" (10 cm) opening closed, sewing as close to the edge as possible.

For Variation 1:

1 Construct the jacket following the steps for Variations 2 and 3, but skip step 2—the pocket for this variation is sewn on after the jacket has been hemmed.

2 Pin a pocket to each front, matching the marks. Topstitch in place along the sides and lower edge, backstitching at the beginning and end to secure.

RICKIE SKIRT

Simple gathered skirt with fitted waist yoke and back zipper in three length variations.

Length Variations

Variation 1: Mini
Photos on pages 76–77

Variation 2: Midi
Photos on pages 72–73, 84, 89, and 92–93

Variation 3: Maxi
Photos on page 91

Supplies
All Variations:

- Lightweight or mid-weight cotton, linen, or silk
- All-purpose thread to match fabric
- 7" (18 cm) zipper
- 1 yard (.9 m) of fusible interfacing in a weight appropriate for your fabric
- Mini, 1¾ yards (1.6 m) of fabric at least 45" (114 cm) wide
- Midi, 2 yards (1.8 m) of fabric at least 45" (114 cm) wide
- Maxi, 2¾ yards (2.5 m) of fabric at least 45" (114 cm) wide

Tools

- Pins
- Scissors
- Water-soluble fabric marker or chalk
- Measuring tape
- Seam ripper

Cutting Instructions
All Variations:

Pattern piece D3, front yoke: cut two from fabric (one will be front yoke and the other will be front yoke facing) and cut one from interfacing
Pattern piece D4, back yoke: cut four from fabric (two will be back yoke and two will be back yoke facing) and cut two from interfacing; also cut two ½" x 7" (1.3 x 18 cm) strips of interfacing
Pattern piece D1, skirt front: cut one from fabric
Pattern piece D2, skirt back: cut two from fabric

Refer to the Pattern Sheet Guide on page 133 to locate the pattern sheet number with the appropriate pieces for your garment. Trace the pattern pieces in your desired size and variation and place them on the fabric per the Cutting Layouts on page 129. Cut out the fabric and transfer any markings from the pattern to the fabric.

All seam allowances are ½" (1.3 cm) unless noted otherwise.

Sewing Instructions
For All Variations:

1 Following the manufacturer's instructions, apply interfacing to the front and back yoke facing pieces.

2 With right sides together, pin the back yoke pieces to the front yoke at the sides, matching notches. Stitch together. Press the seams open; repeat with the yoke facings.

3 With right sides together, matching notches, sew the skirt back pieces to the skirt front.

4 With right sides together, matching notches, sew the skirt back pieces together below the dot.

5 Machine baste a separate line of gathering stitches on each skirt back piece and the skirt front, ⅜" (1 cm) from the top edge of skirt—do not make a continuous line of basting stitches. The basting thread will break if you try to gather too much fabric at once, so it's best to gather in sections.

STEP 4

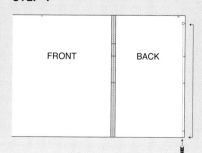

FRONT   BACK

STEP 6

STEP 9

STEP 12

6 With right sides together, pin the yoke to the skirt, matching notches and side seams. Gather the skirt front and skirt back to match the yoke. Adjust the gathers evenly within each section. Stitch. Press the yoke over the seam allowances.

7 To stabilize the zipper opening on each back yoke piece, apply the interfacing strips to the wrong side of the fabric, following the manufacturer's instructions.

8 With right sides still facing, baste the back opening of the skirt and yoke together above the dot. Press the seam open.

9 Place the zipper facedown on the yoke, centered over the back seam. Place the top zipper stop ⅛" (3 mm) below the waist seamline. Hand baste the zipper to the skirt back. Turn the skirt right-side out.

10 Using a zipper foot, topstitch ¼" (6 mm) away from the center seam down one side of the zipper, across the bottom of the zipper (making sure to clear the bottom zipper stop), and back up the other side. Remove all basting stitches.

11 Press under ½" (1.3 cm) on the long edge of the yoke facing. With right sides together, pin the yoke facing to the yoke, matching the notches and side seams; the facing will extend ½" (1.3 cm) past the zipper opening on each side. Stitch. Press the yoke facing over the seam allowances. Press under ½" (1.3 cm) on the sides of the facing.

12 Turn the yoke facing to the inside and press. Tuck the excess zipper tape between the facing and the yoke. Slip stitch the facing to the yoke along the zipper opening, making sure to clear the zipper. Slip stitch the facing to the yoke along the seamline, covering the seam allowance.

13 Hem as desired. Depending on the fabric, you may consider several options: a visible machine hem might be appropriate for a cotton fabric, while a narrow invisible hem stitched by hand or by machine might suit a silk fabric. For either, first press under ¼" (6 mm) to the wrong side and then press under the depth of hem desired. Stitch along the folded edge by machine or slip stitch by hand.

Accessories

STINA EVERY DAY TOTE BAG

Simple tote bag in two sizes with a gusset and a fold-over flap closure.

Variations

Variation 1: Small tote
8" (20 cm) wide x 10" (25 cm) tall (folded height)
Photos on page 79

Variation 2: Large tote
13½" (34 cm) wide x 12½" (32 cm) tall (folded height)
Photos on page 78

Supplies

- Midweight to heavyweight cotton, linen, or denim
- All-purpose thread to match fabric
- 1½" (4 cm) swivel hook and D-ring, 2 sets for each bag
- Small tote, ½ yard (.5 m) of fabric at least 45" (114 cm) wide; if using midweight fabric, 1 yard (.9 m) of fusible buckram for interfacing
- Large tote, ¾ yard (.7 m) of fabric at least 45" (114 cm) wide; if using midweight fabric, 1¼ yards (1.2 m) of fusible buckram for interfacing
- Optional lining fabric, ¼ yard (.3 m) of fabric at least 45" (114 cm) wide for small tote or ½ yard (.5 m) of fabric at least 45" (114 cm) wide for large tote

Tools

- Pins
- Scissors
- Water-soluble fabric marker or chalk
- Ruler, yardstick, or measuring tape

Cutting instructions (no pattern pieces)

Variation 1:

Bag body: Cut one piece of fabric 9" (23 cm) wide by 32" (81.3 cm) long, and if using midweight fabric, cut one piece of buckram to the same dimensions
Bag straps: Cut two pieces of fabric each 2½" (6.5 cm) wide by 38" (96.5 cm) long, and if using midweight fabric, cut one piece of buckram 1½" x 32" (4 x 81.3 cm)
D-ring loop: Cut one piece of fabric 3¼" (8.3 cm) wide by 4" (10 cm) long
Optional bag lining: Cut one piece of fabric 9" (23 cm) wide by 30" (78.7 cm) long

Variation 2:

Bag body: Cut one piece of fabric 14½" (37 cm) wide by 39" (99 cm) long, and if using midweight fabric, cut one piece of buckram to the same dimensions
Bag straps: Cut two pieces of fabric 2½" (6.5 cm) wide by 38" (96.5 cm) long, and if using midweight fabric, cut one piece of buckram 1½" x 32" (4 x 81.3 cm)
D-ring loop: Cut one piece of fabric 3¼" (8.3 cm) wide by 4" (10 cm) long
Optional bag lining: cut one piece of fabric 14½" (37 cm) wide by 37" (96.5 cm) long

NOTE: The finished length of the strap on each bag is 32" (81.3 cm), but the strap can be made shorter or longer depending on your preference; add 6" (15 cm) to your preferred final length to accommodate the hardware.

STEP 2

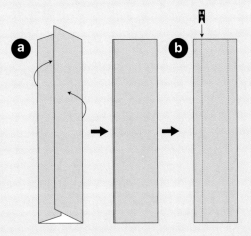

STEP 5

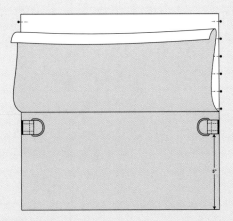

**Sewing Instructions
For All Variations:**

1 If you are using a midweight fabric, follow the manufacturer's instructions to fuse the buckram to the wrong side of the bag body piece.

2 Fold the D-ring loop into thirds, so it is roughly 1⅛" x 4" (2.9 x 10 cm) (a). Topstitch ¼" (6 mm) away from each long folded edge (b). (If you are using a midweight fabric, you may want to interface the loop.) Note that the raw edge should be on the wrong side of the loop when it is wrapped around the D-ring.

3 Cut this piece into two pieces that are roughly 1⅛" x 2" (2.9 x 5 cm). Machine zigzag stitch the raw edges.

4 Fold each piece in half and slide a D-ring into the fold, then stitch as close to the ring as possible; if desired, use a zipper foot or adjust the needle position on your machine if this option is available.

For Variation 1:

5 Fold the long sides of the bag body with right sides facing and pin together, placing the D-ring loops 5" (13 cm) from the top edge on each side, raw edges to the seam allowance with the loops inside the bag. Using a ½" (1.3 cm) seam allowance, stitch each side, back-stitching over the D-ring loops as you go to reinforce. Machine zigzag stitch or serge the seam allowance to finish the edges and prevent fraying.

6 To make the gusset in the bottom of the bag, make a mark in the seam allowance 1" (2.5 cm) up from the bottom on each side. Finger-press a fold along the bottom edge of the bag.

7 Pull the bottom corners apart so that the side seam and the fold on the bottom edge meet, creating a point at each bottom corner.

8 Push the seam allowance to one side. Draw a line across each corner at the mark you made in step 6; each line should be 2" (5 cm) wide (a). Stitch across the line at each corner (b).

9 Trim off the triangle, leaving a ½" (1.3 cm) seam allowance. Machine zigzag stitch the raw edges.

For Variation 2:

10 Fold the long sides of the bag body with right sides facing. Pin together as shown in step 5 but place the D-rings loops 6" (15 cm) from the top edge on each side for this variation, raw edges to the seam allowance with the loops inside the bag. Using a ½" (1.3 cm) seam allowance, stitch each side, backstitching over the D-ring loops as you go to reinforce. Machine zigzag stitch or serge the seam allowance to finish the edges and prevent fraying.

11 To make the gusset in the bottom of the bag, make a mark in the seam allowance 1½" (4 cm) up from the bottom on each side. Finger-press a fold along the bottom edge of the bag.

12 Pull the bottom corners apart so that the side seam and the fold on the bottom edge meet, creating a point at each bottom corner.

13 Push the seam allowance to one side. Referring to the illustration for step 8, draw a line across the corner at the mark you made in step 11; note that each line should be 3" (7.5 cm) wide for this variation. Stitch across the line at each corner.

STEP 8

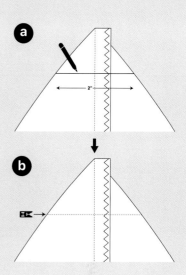

a

2"

b

125

STEPS 18–19

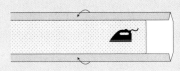

STEP 21

a

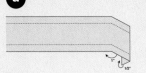

b

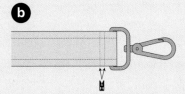

14 Trim off the triangle, leaving a ½" (1.3 cm) seam allowance. Machine zigzag stitch the raw edges.

Optional Lining for All Variations:

15 If you are making a lined bag, repeat steps 5–9 in lining fabric for Variation 1 or repeat steps 10–14 in lining fabric for Variation 2, but note that no D-ring loops will be installed in the lining.

16 Insert the lining into the bag with wrong sides together; the top of the lining will fall 1" (2.5 cm) below the top edge of the bag.

All Variations:

17 Press under ½" (1.3 cm) on the top raw edge and then turn under another ½" (1.3 cm) and press. Stitch close to the first fold. (If you have put a lining in, the raw edge of the lining should be hidden under the second fold).

18 Following the manufacturer's instructions, apply the interfacing to one strap piece, centering it in the middle of both the length and the width, leaving ½" (1.3 cm) on each long side and 3" (7.6 cm) on each short edge that will not be interfaced.

19 Fold under ½" (1.3 cm) on each long side of both strap pieces.

20 With wrong sides together, pin the strap pieces together. Stitch ⅛" to ¼" (3 to 6 mm) away from each edge.

21 Fold under ½" (1.3 cm) on each end of the strap and press, then fold under another 1" (2.5 cm) and press (a). Slide the hook piece into the fold and stitch close to the first fold, then stitch again ¼" (6 mm) away from the first line of stitching (b). Clip the strap to the D-rings.

HEADBAND

Photos on pages 81, 88, 89

Supplies

- A strip of fabric, 10" x 36" (25.4 cm x 91.4 cm)
- Thin gauge wire 35" (88.9 cm) long

Tools

- Pliers
- Matching thread

Instructions

1 Fold the fabric in half lengthwise, right sides facing.

2 Sew a ½" (1.3 cm) seam along the fold, creating a tube.

3 Insert the wire in the tube.

4 Sew the other long side together, using a ½" (1.3 cm) seam allowance. Next, turn the band inside out.

5 Fold under ½" (1.3 cm) on each of the short ends, then topstitch to secure. And you are done: effortless, swift, and fun!

SCARF

Well scarves, super-duper easy to make, and I wanted to include a note about them here as a reminder to you . . . to make scarves! I have many, in all kinds of colors and patterns, and they are usually square. Medium and small ones for my head, larger ones around my neck.

Photo on page 80

Supplies

- Fabric, in the material and size of your choice

Here are some of my favorite sizes:

Scarf: 36 x 36" (91 x 91 cm)

Scarf: 26 x 26" (66 x 66 cm)

Bandana: 20 x 20" (51 x 51 cm)

I also really like the ideas of patterned pocket squares— 11 x 11" (28 x 28 cm)—for that day I get a suit.

Instructions

The sewing is so basic, it's silly to call these instructions: Cut the fabric to the size you would like, plus ⅛" to ¼" (3 to 6 mm) all the way around. Turn the edges under, press, and topstitch to finish.

This a great project for leftover fabric: Scarves are the perfect fashion accessory, especially on bad hair days ;)

CUTTING LAYOUTS

BILLIE TOP (3/4 SLEEVES)

BILLIE TUNIC (SLEEVELESS)

FOR 3/4 VERSION, PLACE
SLEEVE AS FOR BILLIE TOP

MAAR DRESS (SLEEVELESS)

MAAR DRESS (CAP SLEEVES)

MAAR DRESS (3/4 SLEEVES)

PYM PANTS

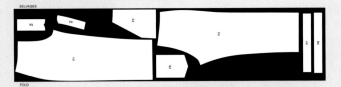

KIKO ROBE (ANKLE LENGTH)

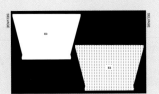

KIKO ROBE (KNEE LENGTH)

KIKO JACKET

RICKIE SKIRT (MINI AND MIDI)

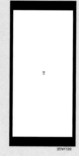

RICKIE SKIRT (MAXI)

RUI SHIRT

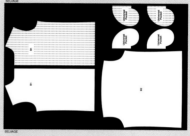

RUI SHIRTDRESS (KNEE LENGTH)

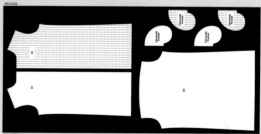

RUI SHIRTDRESS (ANKLE LENGTH)

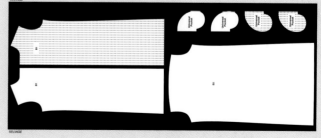

PATTERN SHEET GUIDES

BILLIE TOP/TUNIC
Pattern Sheets 1 & 3
Pattern Sheet 5 (pocket)

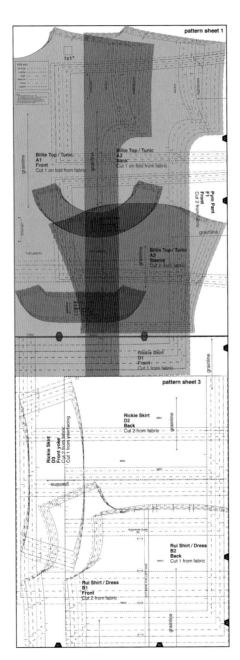

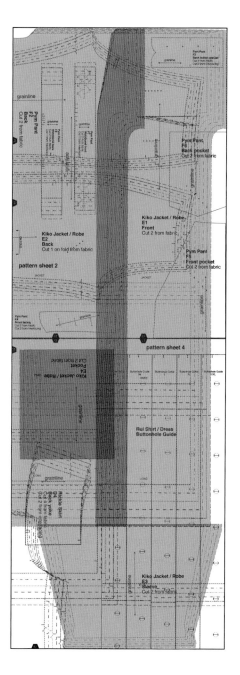

KIKO JACKET/ROBE
Pattern Sheets 2 & 4

2

4

PYM PANTS

Pattern Sheets 1 & 2

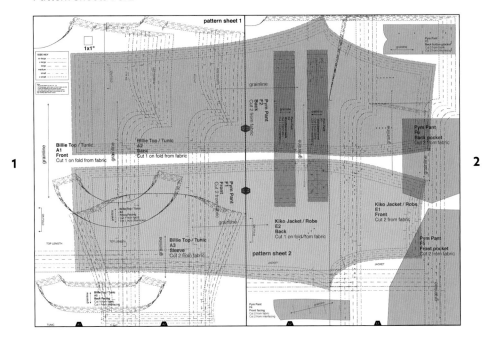

RICKIE SKIRT
Pattern Sheets 3 &4

3

4

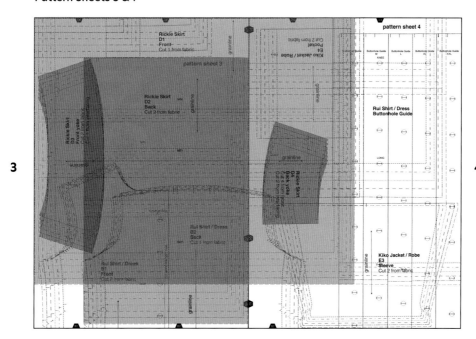

MAAR DRESS
Pattern Sheets 5 & 6

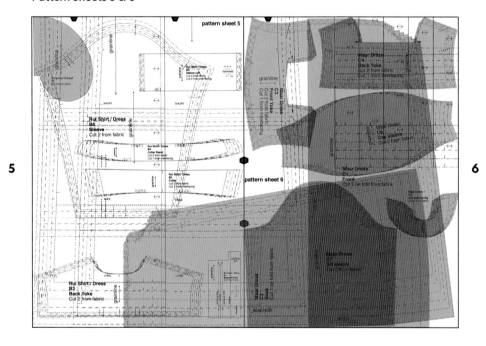

RUI SHIRT/DRESS
Pattern Sheets 3, 4, 5 & 6

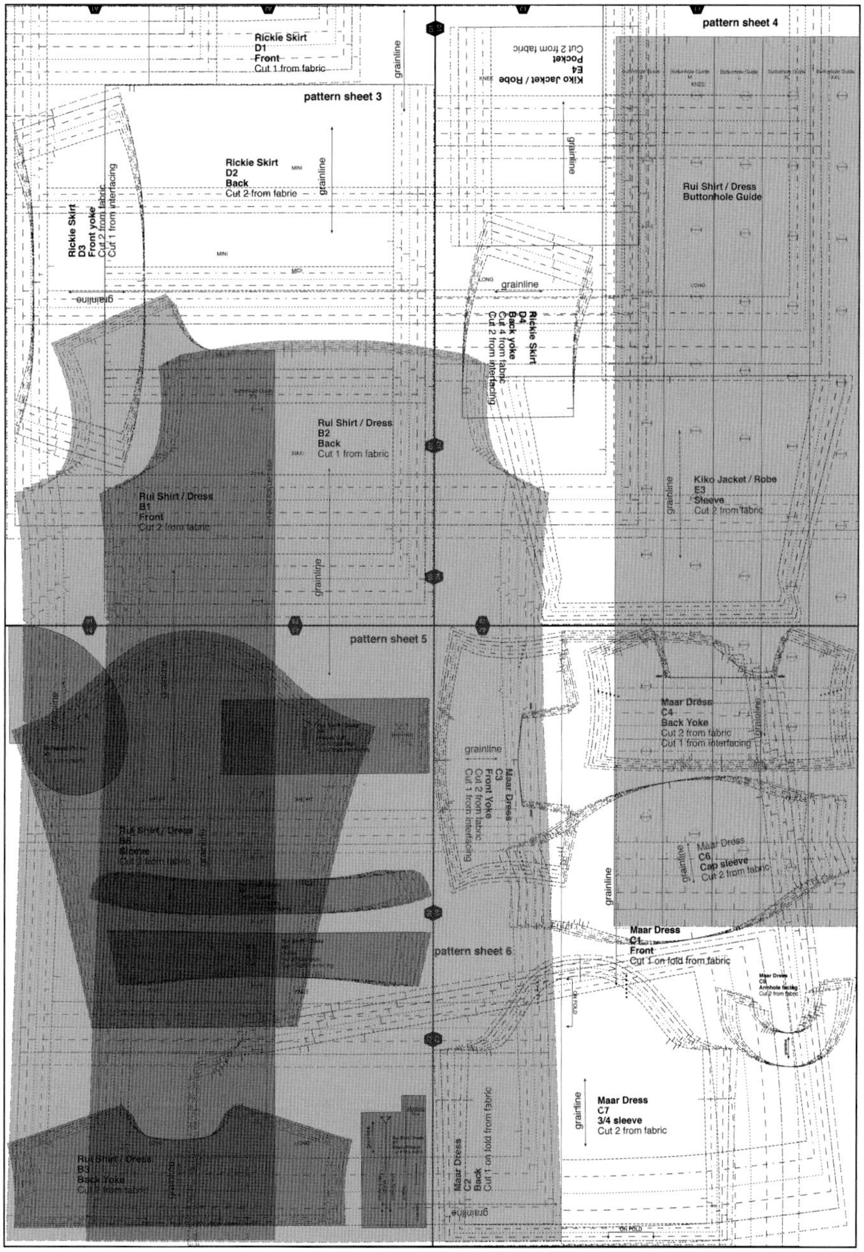

3

4

5

6

ABOUT THE AUTHOR

Some of you might have discovered my work and my company Lotta Jansdotter through sewing, by using my cotton quilt fabrics. Some of you bought my stationery and paper products that were created with Chronicle Books more than fifteen years ago. Some of you bought my fabric calendars, linen pillows, and bags I produced and sold out of my shop in San Francisco. And many of you have read my books and attended my print workshops and retreats.

Either way, I wanted to share with you a bit more about my work and my process. I have been so fortunate to work with many different companies since my start in 1996. I have created porcelain dining sets, bedding, rugs, children's toys, towels, thermoses, melamine tableware, laptop covers, luggage, wrapping paper, washi tapes, and much, much more—and for the past eight years I have happily created collections of quilting cotton fabrics.

Last year, I started to feel a big shift in how I wanted to continue my work. Coming up on the twenty-fifth anniversary of Lotta Jansdotter I found myself wanting to simplify and return to feeling closer and connected to the production of my products—as I did when I first began. I wanted to have more creative control over colors and materials, and to have more intimate, meaningful relationships with my manufacturers and customers. So I decided to go back to producing small, special, and limited collections of products and fabrics again, just as I did when I started Lotta Jansdotter in 1996. It feels really exciting to come back to this way again.

It is important for me to have my fabrics screen printed or properly offset printed. Digitally printed fabrics are certainly much more cost-effective, and would be much easier for me to produce, but at the time of writing this book, I don't find the print quality can compare in detail or quality to screen printed fabrics. Perhaps one day they will be, and I am very open to that, but until then I choose to work with smaller companies that can still offer handprinted production. I am delighted to be working with organizations in India, Africa, and eastern Europe that produce my fabrics in very small batches by printing them by hand and at the same time can offer fair terms of employment and empower local communities through this creative work.

The Billie Tunic with
Pym Pants

137

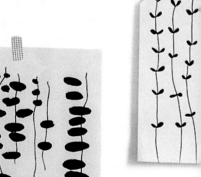

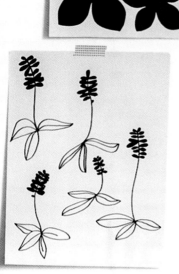

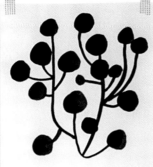

CREATING MY DESIGNS AND ARTWORK

I make my designs by hand. I draw motifs with brushes and India ink and cut shapes out of black paper with scissors until I discover ideas that I am drawn to. After that, I use a fat marker pen or a wax crayon to make many marks on thick paper and then carve the shape in a rubber block, which I print in many directions until I find a repeat I like (the whole time getting rubber cement on my hands and ink and Wite-Out under my nails).

Most times I know what motif or shape I want, but sometimes I don't know where the design will end up; it is a journey in itself. I use a copy machine to scale design elements up and down, bigger and smaller, then cut them out and move them around until I have a layout that feels right. I glue it all down with rubber cement. Or I roll out a piece of paper on the floor and draw with big brushes, creating strokes or shapes. Sometimes things come out that I truly don't want, and do not look like anything I am drawn to. But do it enough times and eventually you create something that gives a spark. And it sticks. This process uses a lot of paper, but I save all the scraps and leftovers and sometimes I cut those up—and all of a sudden the scraps become a new design.

The next step involves bringing my designs to a plotter and scanning it all in digitally. I do have assistants (rather patient ones) who help me clean up the designs and apply my chosen colors until we have final digital files This whole process can be so messy and so slow at times, and I let it—I wouldn't have it any other way. I love being involved in every step, in the moment with messy hands touching real materials and hearing the paper crinkle. This is how I always have done it and always probably will.

This process of creating designs and art by hand makes me happy and calm. It is what I have done for the last twenty-five years and it will probably be how I do it the next twenty-five.

A very rewarding and delightful part of this process is that the creation doesn't stop: The fabric designs come alive into projects and garments that you make, each individual and unique on its own.

ACKNOWLEDGMENTS

TUSEN TACK! (Thousands of Thank Yous)

Felicity: You are so talented, delightful, special, sweet, and such a dear to me. I appreciate all your patience and resourcefulness (and your always excellent tips and suggestions for everything fabulous, inspiring, and tasty). I am so happy to get to work with you on this book.

Agnetha: You moved mountains for me, with all your excellent sewing on this giant project. Without your help this book would not have gotten done. *Tusen Tack kära svägerska.*

Jenny: You are simply the best! It is not always easy, but it is always so, so good. Thank you for your beautiful work. You are an amazing photographer and such a dear friend.

To all my lovely family and friends, the models, you make this book just perfect and very special: Selah, Heather, Andrew, Linnea, Judy, Tiina, Mattias, Margaretha, Teo, Brent, Cherokee, Ellie, Felicity, Alejandra, Boris, Olga, Jenny, Tim, and Agnetha.

Skilled hands that helped me with even more sewing: Thank you, Daniela, Mohamad (SYrien) and Z Skrädderi.

Thank you, Purl Soho, for donating such beautiful materials and fabrics for this book. I appreciate all your support for so many years. It means the world to me.

TUSEN TACK Isobel (and Bryr), and Mickey (and Sabah) for making my very favorite shoes that I wear ALL the TIME!

Madi: For helping me make these fabric prints come alive on fabric.

Mark: Appreciate extra hands with equipment, for hosting us in your lovely and creative home, and for all your support.

Shawna: For your constant, cheerful encouragement and support, and for believing in my vision and in this book.

Jenice: Thank you so much for your incredible patience and help. I could not have created this book without you and I am so grateful for your talent and your brilliant work. Thank you for helping me make a book that I am very proud and happy about.

Tim: For wonderful meals, constant support, excellent calvados, and the many swims.

August: Thank you for bringing me sunshine and big hugs. Thank you for opening my eyes and mind to new things (and for insisting on me doing those damned ten push-ups every day). You make me very, very proud.

Nick: All your love is everything.

RESOURCES

PATTERNED FABRIC

I designed all of the patterned and printed fabrics used in the book; they are from my line of linen, linen-cotton, and blends in different weights of fabrics for garment, home décor, and craft sewing. You can find available fabrics at www.jansdotter.com

You can, of course, email if you have any questions about my fabrics.

questions@jansdotter.com

SOLID FABRIC

All the non-printed, solid fabrics in this book come from my favorite fabric shop, Purl Soho in New York. Purl has a well-curated selection of wonderful, great quality fabric in an amazing range of color choices. They have an online shop, but if you ever find yourself in New York, I recommend a visit to their shop; it is such a special and inspiring place, don't miss it.

www.purlsoho.com
459 Broome Street
New York, New York 1001

NOTIONS, RIBBONS, AND TRIM

I am lucky to live close to New York City and the garment district, where you can find many small, independent shops specializing in notions and trim of different kinds. I am all in favor of supporting local shops close to you, and, of course, the big, vast internet is also there for you to shop for what you need.

My friend Felicity also likes to source fabric and notions from:

Cloth House London
www.clothhouse.com
30 Royal College St, London NW1 0TA, United Kingdom

The Fabric Store
https://weare.thefabricstoreonline.com

Fancy Tiger Crafts
59 Broadway, Denver, CO 80203
www.fancytigercrafts.com

Tessuti Fabrics
110 Commonwealth St
Surry Hills NSW 2010
02 9211 5536
https://www.tessuti-shop.com/pages/about-tessuti

CLOG

My absolute favorite clog is made by Bryr, a small independent company based in San Francisco. It was started by my brilliant and dear friend Isobel. She and I met twenty-four years ago, when we did trunk shows together in art galleries around town (and had the best time peddling our goods while socializing, having a beer or two, and bartering special things we made). Please visit Isobel's clog company to find the coolest and most comfortable clogs there are. (I can even walk in a heel, when it is a clog!)

www.bryrstudio.com

SABAH SHOES

Another one of my favorite companies. I simply love their company culture and their products:
I have four different pairs, and still want more. These simple Turkish peasant shoes (still handmade in Turkey) are super comfortable and pair easily with almost any outfit. Sabahs come in all kinds of happy, timeless, stylish colors, and sometimes patterns.

Please visit their shop and say "hi" to Mickey, the proprietor, from me.

www.sabah.am

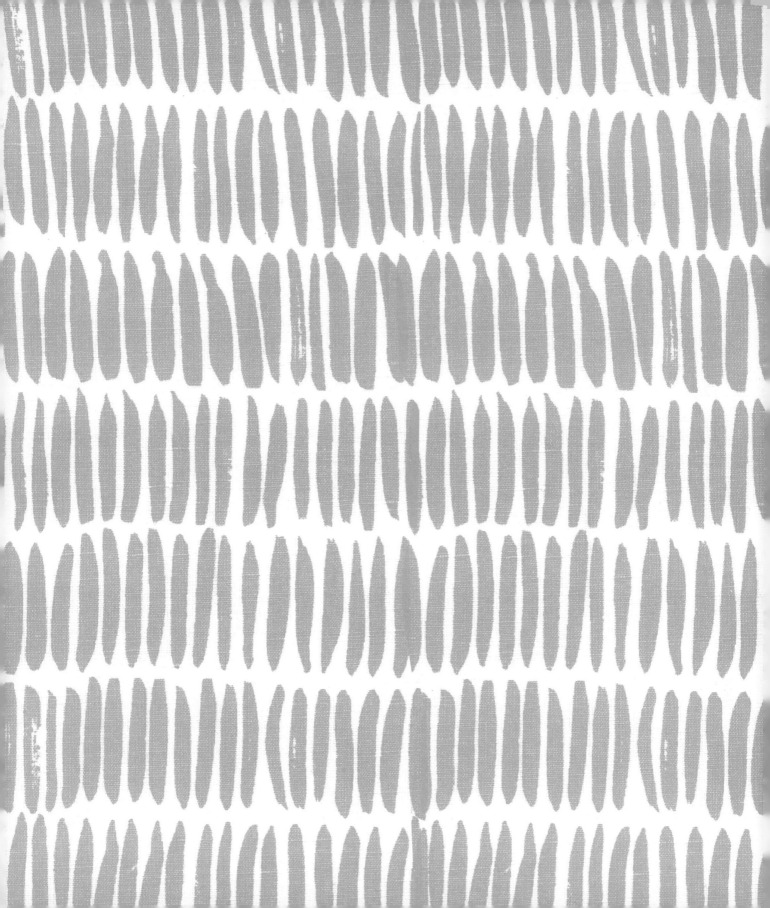

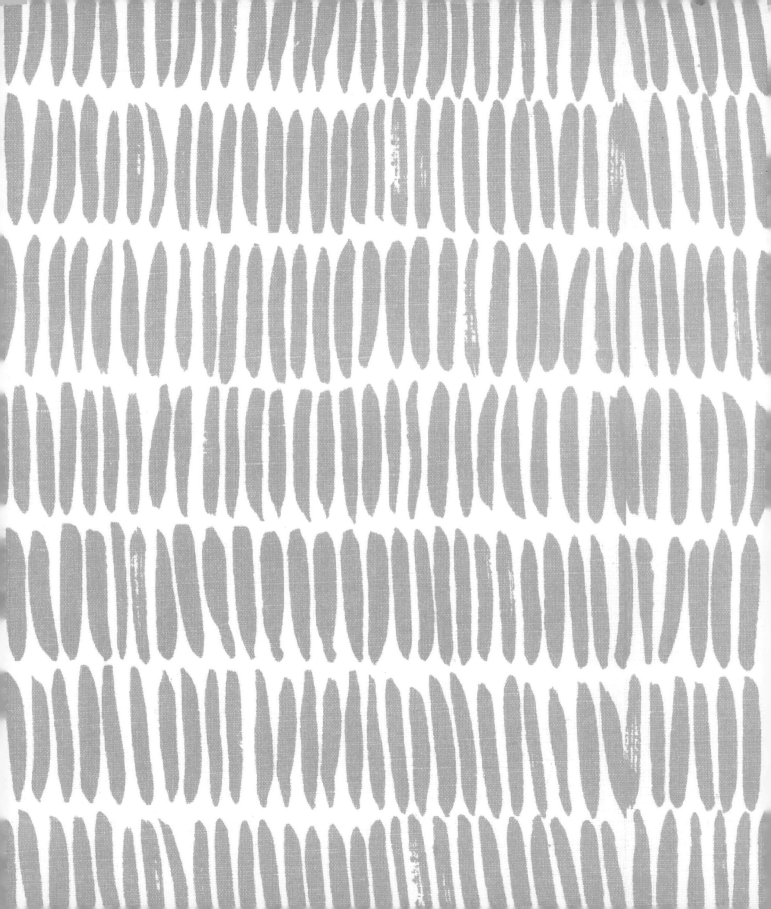